THE HUNGER TO GROW

Retire? "No, I'm still hungry.
What's for dessert?"

Talents
Passions
Enjoyments

How to Enjoy the Dessert Years of Your Life

Peter H Nicholls

The Hunger To Grow

Copyright © 2016 Peter H Nicholls
Adelaide, Australia

Cover Design – Candice Leathem

Published 2016 by DoctorZed Publishing
10 Vista Ave, Skye, South Australia 5072
www.doctorzed.com

ISBN: 978-0-9945542-3-9 (print book)
ISBN: 978-0-9945542-2-2 (ebook)

This book is copyright. Apart from fair dealings for the purposes of private study, research, criticism or review, as permitted under the Copyright Act, no part may be reproduced by any process without written permission from the author or publisher.

Layout design by Anna Dimasi
Printed

Dedication

This book is dedicated to my many teachers who, over the whole of my life, have appeared (and continue to appear) when the student is ready. You have opened so many doors for me, for which I shall be eternally grateful. Each of your contributions have made me a better person, encouraging me to develop my talents, unlock my passions and move out of my comfort zone in ways that I would otherwise have never dreamed of doing. Because of you I continue to enjoy the sweet life of my dessert years – a life that still satisfies my voracious hunger to keep on growing.

Other Titles

*Enjoy Being You –
How Leisure Can Help You Become the Person You Want to Be*

*How to Create Your Second Adulthood –
Planning your transition from full time work to 'whatever is next in your life'*

*Enjoy Being Proud of Who You Are:
52 Inspirational Life-Skills Messages for Teenagers*

*How sweet life is when your developed
talents and passions satisfy your hunger to grow.*

Preface

The whole of your life from birth to death – not just your working career life – is a continuum of progress, growth and self-actualisation. It is what nature always intended of you. But ever since the work ethic came into vogue at least a couple of hundred years ago, we have had drummed into us the belief that life, growth and development starts and ends with our working careers. Respected dictionaries still define 'retire' with terms like withdraw (from life?), retreat (into your shell?), stop (living?), and go back (to the past?).

One of the refreshing advances in 21st century society is that we have at last swept away these negative and limiting perspectives on when and how our lives grow, flourish and blossom. In my lifestyle mentoring business I searched for a new more positive phrase and came up with "what's for dessert? I've finished the main course and I'm still hungry". This phrase says it all.

Even that expression may just be a sign of the times. Baby boomers may well be the last generation to experience life in the traditional three stages – preparation for your working life - your working life and then a life after your working years. It happens already with eating – we no longer limit ourselves to a sitting of entrée, main course and dessert. We eat what we like when we like. Our perception of our traditional journey through life is going the same way with people deciding when and for how long they will work and in whatever order suits their thinking. We are beginning to live life on our own terms. No longer is life centred on work, though of course work still serves a vital role in giving structured economic and social value to our lives and the community that our work serves.

What do you want to do in your dessert years? What will be the unique ingredients in your recipe? You certainly want it to taste great, contains large dollops of passion, full of rich experiences, keeps you healthy and, best of all, satisfies your hunger to keep on moving forward, growing in mind, body and spirit, enjoyed to the last drop.

We live in a rapidly-changing, highly mobile society where individual creativity, innovation, challenge and the desire to keep moving forward is becoming the norm. Age means little now in our natural desire to unleash our talents, passions and potential. Structured work is only one way to achieve this. We are increasingly realizing that work goals limit us to the demands and expectations of bosses and clients. Life after the end of our working career frees us to express ourselves in our ways for our reasons and for our own unique personal sense of satisfaction.

The dessert years however are less about a period of time in your life. More they are about a change in your attitude towards what, for you, life is all about. The dessert years begin when you start thinking about (and gradually act on) a transition in your life's priorities from doing what you *have* to do (supported by what you *love* to do) to doing what you *love* to do (supported by what you *have* to do). For most of us that transition begins to take place long before any thought of quitting paid employment. Usually it starts somewhere between the ages of forty-five to fifty-five.

Setting The Stage

Imagine you are attending a live theatre performance divided into three Acts. It is interval, following the conclusion of the second Act and you are reflecting on the show so far. You feel that Acts One and Two have been powerful and thought-provoking. You are wondering what surprises the rest of the show might bring.

But this show is unique. There is only one performance…it is a play written by you and you are writing the script as the performance happens in real time…the actors are on stage waiting for their lines. There is no rehearsal and there is only performance – this is opening night and closing night all in one. And no one yet knows – not even you, the playwright – what the ending will be. And the final twist? You are the lead actor, the star of the show.

The play is called "Your Life".

Act One embraced the early years of your life – the years that prepared you for work. The content of Act Two has been your working life. Act Three is yet to come and you wonder what surprises it has in store for you. Act Three may well be a long one. It's up to you to make it memorable for you and for those who love you. You will want to feel that, at the end of "Your Life", the rest of the cast and the audience alike will give you a standing ovation, acknowledging that you have given a performance they will never forget.

You have of course written many sub-plots along the way – getting a job, getting married, having children, retiring from competitive sport, adjusting to the kids leaving home, to name but a few. So in one sense the prospect of giving up fulltime work is just another sub-plot that you will have managed to live and grow through, just as you did through all the previous life changes. This one might seem different because work has been the centre of your life for so many years. Your job has defined who you are – in your eyes and in the eyes of everybody else in your life – at work, home and even at play.

Many people can't wait to retire. You may perhaps have seen work as of little more value than enabling you to pay the bills. A few good things have happened and there were times when you really enjoyed it, but by and large you find work to be a necessity rather than a joy. On the other hand you may have embraced work as a key part of your personal life evolution, to the point that you don't want to quit. This is especially the case if you have built up your own business and see it as your primary driver for living. You can't envisage a life that doesn't involve a working career.

I have mentioned two scenarios. Your experience might be somewhere in between.

Whatever you feel about work you will have done some financial planning for your later years. We all spend considerable time and money to make sure we have financial security during our dessert years. It's just as important to develop your own self-investment plan. A self-investment plan is exactly what it says – investing in your own interests, talents, abilities, passions and dreams – deciding what you actually want to do with your time in the next phase of your life. Statistically speaking, we can look forward to living a lot longer than people did in past generations. In the times of the 19th century Industrial Revolution, management felt you had lived most of your life by the age of 65 and likely to die by age 70. There was little point to planning a full and meaningful life after your working years then. Now you might even live as long yet as your working life so far. That's a long time if you are thinking of spending your dessert years basically sitting in your rocking chair watching the world go by.

Whatever your feelings are about this final stage of your life, fear can be a big factor in your thinking. Not just fear of not having enough money to enjoy your dessert years but also the fear of a life without work. Will you have interests that motivate you in the way your career work has done over the years? You will need to make some long-term lifestyle decisions in a fast-moving, rapidly-changing era where it is hard to predict what the world will be like next week or next year, let alone over the rest of your life. Will you just keep going the way you are for all those years? Probably not.

Your way of thinking about retirement is being influenced by many factors other than simply the role of work in your life and your identity as a person. Whether you are male or female, you will be experiencing a change-of-life. You might be starting to wonder if your life is like a glass that is half-full and still filling, or a glass that is half-empty and continuing to drain away. You are certainly starting to see almost everything differently – including your priorities, your physical and mental abilities, your financial needs and who is important in your life. To many of us these changes are scary because they are signs of getting old. Increasingly though, we are starting to see this changed outlook on life as something of a release from the expectations we felt were placed on us in the first half of our lives. Maturity is helping us to realize not only are we entitled to follow our passions but others actually want us to relax and be ourselves more.

Putting it simply, you are moving into a wonderful stage of life where you start the gradual process of changing the emphasis from:

- Making what you *have* to do the centre of your life (supported by what you *love* to do)....to

- Making what you love to do as the centre of your life (supported by what you have to do).

It doesn't happen overnight but the very thought will drive you onwards over the coming years.

They say everything happens in three's and that applies to life itself.

I have already described your life is like a traditional three-course meal. The other three-stage perspective relates to a statement I made very early in this book: "The whole of your life from birth to death – not just your working career life – is a continuum of progress, growth and self-actualisation."

1. Where you are at right now in your life's progress, growth and self-actualization

2. What interests/passions you would like still to pursue towards fulfilling your natural-born potential

3. What actions/changes/recalibrations you might make in your desire to fulfil that potential

Now, long before you make any decisions whether to cease fulltime work, is a great time to seriously think about those three statements and how this book can help you look ahead positively and with optimism to the promise of your life still to come.

What's For Dessert

By the time you are in your late 50's society is giving you all sorts of encouragements to start thinking about that word retirement. Perhaps those years of paying superannuation contributions can soon legally become available to you. Perhaps it is just a feeling of "how many more years do I want to keep doing this". Whatever the prompt may be you are increasingly conscious of the need to make some big decisions about what you want to do with the rest of your life.

It's not unlike the feeling you get when you are getting down to the last few mouthfuls of the main course of a meal. You are starting to think, *"I have enjoyed the main course but now I am looking forward to choosing a dessert"*. As I suggested earlier:

"What's for dessert??
I've finished the main course and I'm still hungry".

You constantly have a want to eat food in order to satisfy your hunger. Once you have eaten, you feel temporarily satisfied. But there is another hunger which is never satisfied – the hunger to keep growing, developing your talents, enriching your life and achieving your deepest wants. I call it your life-hunger, the hunger that drives you forward in the best and worst situations, unstoppable until your last breath or the onset of a health condition that overrides that desire.

Your life-hunger sometimes causes you to take little bites, sometimes big bites and there are even times when you might bite off more than you can chew. Life comes back to bite you at times too, but you never lose that innate desire to keep on moving forward in life, growing, flourishing and blossoming. Thinking of your future not as retirement but as enjoying your dessert years heralds the beginning of a new era in which age has no bearing on your outlook on life. The issue of whether or not to keep working will be influenced less by economics and more by your hunger to keep on growing as a person.

How to keep satisfying your hunger to make the most of your personal life potential will continue to be as it has always been - the product of your own unique mix of natural-born talents and passions, garnished with your personal life experiences. Prepared and served in your own way you can produce a lifetime culinary delight that no other chef has created in human history, nor will there be anyone in the future with your particular life ingredients, talents and passions to create quite the same masterpiece.

The Value of Dessert

Say you are enjoying a night out for dinner with family or friends. Your main course was very satisfying and it was also a responsible choice with a good balance of vegetables, and perhaps some fish, red meat or other ingredients that are generally recognized as 'being good for you'. Someone suggests that you all have a dessert. There is an enthusiastic yes from around the table. Clearly everyone feels that they have done the right thing with their main course and now it's time to have something that is going to taste great and will be fun to eat.

The menu indicates that there is a wide variety of dessert options from which to choose. Do you choose on the basis of cost? Or do you, within a reasonable context of your available budget, let your imagination run riot as you anticipate having something that you are going to really love eating? Your taste-buds begin salivating as you savour the expectation of how good your dessert will taste, with just the right (to you) texture, colour, aroma and flavour. Everyone around the table is delighting in the fact that they enjoy the right to choose exactly which dessert they want without regard to their normal eating rules or what anyone else is going to choose. There may well be a happy discussion about which each person has chosen.

The experts tell us that while all this is going on, the brain is having a great deal to do with the process. It is exercising your senses of taste, smell, touch, vision, memory of past experiences, and mixing all of these sensations to come up with an answer to the question of what you think you would like to have for dessert. We are told that such decisions – even our choice of dessert - can reflect so much of what we love about life and have done so since the day we were born.

At the conclusion of the meal there is a sense of relaxed satisfaction as the group reflects on how much they enjoyed their meal, especially the dessert. Yes the cost was a factor but the tastes, the richness of the experience and the extent to which they enjoyed themselves was uppermost in their minds. And your choice took into account any impact the experience would have on your continuing health and vitality...didn't it.

All that to decide on something that is going to satisfy your food hunger for a matter of minutes. What sort of life choices might you come up with if you used this wonderfully-creative, imaginative, personal, individual process for enjoying your dessert years? Nor do you have to make decisions that are going to last for the whole of your remaining life. You can order dessert as often as you wish, just so long as each new decision gives you continuing satisfaction in your hunger to grow, develop and stay fit – mentally, physically and spiritually.

The fact that your food taste buds can reflect so much of your life has equal relevance when it comes to planning what you want to do in your dessert years. We have long understood that everything we do in life can in some way be traced back to our childhood. No matter how revolutionary your dessert years thinking might be compared to your working life, you will always be you and build on your natural growth since birth. You will see more what I mean by this in the later chapter on "My Story".

How much money will you need to enjoy your dessert years? It's a question that dominates the issue of planning for retirement. I find this borne out through a Google Alert I have that gives me a weekly list of online articles from all parts of the world about *Retirement Planning*. Almost always they focus on the financial planning aspects. This was much of the reason behind me writing this book. Not only to get people to think about what they might do in the many years they may statistically-speaking still have ahead of them but to allay many of peoples' fears about retirement. The word fear is sometimes interpreted as an acronym F.E.A.R. – False Expectations Appearing Real.

By law I cannot help you with your financial planning. I am a lifestyle mentor. I would simply and strongly urge you to seek professional financial planning advice specific to your particular financial circumstances. Not that I don't have some views on the nature and role of money during my own dessert years to date. I've often said, tongue-in-cheek, *"if I knew how long I was going to live I'd know how fast to spend my money"*. Since I left the fulltime workforce money has of course continued to be necessary to meet my daily needs and some for the more significant needs like a car and the occasional travel. I have however come to regard money less in terms of the amount I have and more about the nature, the role and priority of the money that I have in getting the greatest value out of my remaining years. It's an excellent time to remember the old saying, *be thankful for what you have rather than regret what you don't have.*

Where Are You In Your Life?

Do you feel your life is on course to achieving your potential, following your passions and maximizing your natural talents? This is always a thought-provoking question, especially in the middle stages of your life. This section of the book will help you to clarify what you need to consider before planning the dessert years of your life.

An Unexpected Death

You hit one of those big 0's – forty, fifty or sixty years of age. (My son was horrified when he reached thirty!) These days they are not big in terms of age – people speak of sixty as the new fifty, fifty as the new forty and so on. They are big years however in terms of their impact on your thinking. You knew you would eventually reach fifty and sixty of course but it is something of a shock when you actually get there. The person looking out at the world through your eyes has never changed in your mind. You look at yourself in the mirror and you only see a person who has matured. You still have your youthful looks – well...you think so anyway - and you are as mentally alert and physically active as you have been for years. Nothing's changed. Or has it?

The truth is that it's often what you can't see that is starting to change. Changes in the way you are thinking, your emotions, your outlook on life, your sense of what seems important in life, even in the way people respond to you. You might suddenly cringe a little when you hear someone refer to 'older people' or people who are showing signs of ageing. Did they have you in mind? Surely not! Yet I remember the absolute shock when for the very first time a school pupil stood up for me in the bus and insisted I take her seat. I should have been thankful but my first reaction was one of horror. *Do I look that old??!* In fact we were both right – she saw signs of my physical ageing, but she couldn't possibly know that in my heart I was continuing to feel mentally young and agile.

Suddenly somebody you know well dies unexpectedly. You have probably already experienced the death of somebody you know. This time however he or she is at an age uncomfortably close to yours. You feel what is often called a *mortality jolt* – a rude reminder that you are indeed mortal. You are staring in the face the fact that one day it will all come to an end. Worst of all you have no idea when it might happen. You certainly didn't expect your friend to die so soon. You still think of yourself as being 'immortal', well at least for quite a few years yet. You don't dwell on this, you just become a little more aware that the *one day* as in 'one day I want to…" is getting closer.

Some years ago a client of mine was hit by a car while he was standing on the footpath. He was in hospital for weeks in a coma and his life was hanging in the balance. When I was finally able to speak with him his first words to me were "Peter whatever you planned to do, do it today". It was a sobering reminder that life is always a delicate balance of, statistically, the modern person can expect to live increasingly longer, against the reality that it could all end today. Personally, it strengthened my resolve to continue making the most of my talents as much as possible for the benefit of as many people as possible and for as long as life would allow me to do so. Put more simply, I had a good look at my bucket list and realized that life is what you are doing right now; there is no guarantee of tomorrow. For me, this book forms part of my continuing resolve, part of which is to do what I can to help you get the most out of that 'single-performance play - "Your Life".

The good news is that this change-of-life going on around you and in your own life includes a new and very positive social shift in reviewing, assessing and resolving the issues affecting your decision about if and when to leave fulltime work. Essentially, we are retiring the word "retired". It's time to take a new, more modern approach to writing your script for your life's Act Three in the play "Your Life". This approach should reflect the realities of what people are in fact thinking and doing to re-energize their lives today.

There has already been a huge shift in the way life's journey is being viewed. The younger generations are already seeing the traditional option of one long and distinguished career at work as just one of a variety of options to consider in deciding how best they can satisfy their hunger to grow and develop their potential. The idea of reaching a specific age at which society decrees that you should stop working for any reason at all is rapidly becoming an outdated way of thinking.

This is a matter of some public debate as governments globally look for ways of managing the increasingly major economic challenges of an ageing society. One option to minimize the impact of this on the economy is to increase the age at which a person is entitled to receive a government-funded age pension. This possibility appals those people who want to quit work as soon as possible and see it as changing the goal posts at a late stage of their life. They were looking to the pension as a key part of sustaining their preferred lifestyle during the dessert years.

Then there are those of us too who will decide if and when to cease formal employment irrespective of what governments decide in relation to the eligibility to receive an age pension. The most public reason is usually that they have made good financial plans well in advance of leaving fulltime work. The lesser understood reason – and I believe at least as important – is that they have seen life as being more than simply their job. They have also developed life-time interests over many years, based on following their passions and developing their natural talents. They have long recognized, whether they like their job or not, that what they do for sheer enjoyment provides emotional and health benefits far beyond simply enjoying a break from work. This book suggests this approach is never too late to adopt and build into your continuing life journey.

Keep On Growing

A tree does not stop growing at age 65, it continues to grow, mature and blossom for the term of its natural life. So it is with us. It is vital therefore to devote a chapter to the fact that, whatever we decide to do about our working career, it's a separate issue to our natural hunger to keep on growing for the full term of our natural lives.

During the often very long years of your working life you have no doubt dreamt about finally having the time to do all the things you love doing, follow your passions, play golf, paint, write, travel, or start an interest that you have been playing around with in your spare time and could fully pursue without worrying about going to work every day. Perhaps you were fortunate enough to enjoy some long service leave from work and loved it, or have enjoyed taking regular annual leave and think that retirement is more of the same. Beware! Retirement is nothing like long service leave or a long holiday, especially these days when the average lifespan is rapidly extending.

Far from being a greater form of long service leave, life after fulltime employment is more like moving to another planet, say Mars, to start a completely new life in an alien community. Many people in fact actually do make a major physical move to a living environment that is totally different to anything they have experienced in their working life. It's popularly referred to as a sea-change or (if you want to escape to the country), a tree-change.

Even if you don't make such a physical move, you have to go back to basics and to re-think everything you thought you knew about life and all that has been sacred to you throughout your working life. Your comfort zone might not be the safe place you thought it was. You will need to make some interesting decisions on what to take with you on your new journey, a journey that is so different that it opens up many opportunities for new excitement in your life. You will also need to decide what to leave behind as excess baggage.

It's important to remember here that a key reason why this book has become necessary is because the idea of retiring at sixty-five was historically based on the expectation you may well be dead by seventy. Since the late 1800s, life expectancy for Australian boys and girls has increased by over 30 years. During 1881-1890, the average life expectancy of a newborn boy was 47.2 years and that of a newborn girl 50.8 years. By 2007-2009, *average* life expectancy had risen to 79.3 years for newborn boys and 83.9 years for newborn girls.[1]

There are now many people continuing to lead full lives, including paid work, into their 90's and some even beyond. There is plenty of serious thinking that the average years of life expectancy will continue to rise, particularly because of the accelerating rate of

---

[1] 4102.0 - Australian Social Trends, Mar 2011 Australian Bureau of Statistics report

medical breakthroughs and understanding of the physiological and psychological needs of an ageing population. I believe – and it has been my personal experience as I move through my seventies – that the mere belief and expectation that we may live much longer than our parents and grandparents does itself add years to our lives, our expectations and our health, especially our mental fitness. I feel sure this line of thinking is a major reason why, when I tell people my age, their consistent reaction is one of disbelief – "I would never have thought you were that old Peter!" (a comment I always happily accept!)

Most importantly, you will have to learn how to overcome one of the biggest problems facing the world-wide ageing population today – the fear of not having regular employment, its steady income, its structures and its emotional benefits on which your life has been grounded since you first started working. There will of course be significant financial implications every step of the way. I re-emphasise my earlier point that such issues need to be fully discussed with a financial planner with whom you feel fully comfortable.

Let's assume you have reached the stage of your life where you would once have been expected – or perhaps been told by your employer – to quit work and "retire". Whoa! Me?? Retire?? All those negative perceptions of retirement that we talked about earlier flood into your mind. The thought of existing without the structure – let alone the consistent flow of money – of a working life can fill you with a sense of fear. But when you think about it, fear of an unknown future has long been a feature of your life to date.

Think of the many times in the past when you had to find the courage to take major steps in your life and succeeded, wondering later what all the fuss was about? Leaving home, getting married, moving interstate or overseas – they are all big moves which you went into with fear and trepidation. It's the same here. The main difference in this case is that it may be the first time in your adult life that you have the opportunity to develop a plan that revolves not around other's demands and expectations. Rather it revolves around you, encouraging you to do your own thing, in your own way, at your own pace to satisfy your own unique dreams and desires.

You've probably never seriously wondered what life might be like for you decades into the future. Your perceptions at this stage can only be based on your past experiences and what you have seen happening in the lives of people many years older than you. But now this is about *your* life, one that is unique to you, your life to date and your life still to come. No two lives are ever the same and only you can decide exactly what you need to remain a content and happy person during the coming years.

What is 'old'?

The well-known actor, the late Jimmy Durante, is purported to have said, on the occasion of his 80th birthday, "*If I had known I was going to live this long. I would have taken better care of myself!*" George Burns was still telling jokes on stage until he was 100. There is one's chronological years of age and the stage of life when one begins to feel old. Any relationship between the two is purely a matter of personal perception. When somebody suggests to you that you should "act your age", they are in fact attempting to impose their perceptions of "age" and "old" on you.

I know of so many people who are well into their 80's and even their 90's who say they are still waiting to get old. The saying '*you are only as old as you feel*' is so true. You don't have to think of planning a life less active than you presently enjoy. You will go on enjoying life just so long as you keep on feeling that you are enjoying life!

Over the years you have at some time have been called old, usually by your children or someone else of a younger generation. Did the comment make you feel old or suggest you should slow down? Of course not. It was only their perception of what life must be like "at your age". And that is exactly what it is – their perception. Ageism issues – the belief of younger people that older people are not capable of keeping up with change, new thinking, new technology and the changing pace of life – are all about perceptions.

I heard such implied remarks at a seminar organised to address issues facing mature workers in government services. The discussions continually came back to the concern (*perceptions*, to me!) that mature-age workers (another politically-correct term for "old") could have difficulty coping with the rapidly-changing technology. I stood the comments until I could stand them no more. The seminar was almost at a close when I asked if I could speak. I told the largely-young delegates that I was over seventy, still running a business with a complex website and making effective use of many forms of social media through which to promote my business. I generally explained that I was probably way ahead of many younger people when it came to dealing with the new technology. Interestingly I received rousing applause and the seminar moderator came over and shook my hand enthusiastically. I tend to think the feeling of the seminar delegates was one of relief – relief that they could look forward to the prospect of still having a busy, active and rewarding life even after they turn 70.

By the time you have finished this book you will be a long way down the track to creating in your mind a personal life plan that suits and expresses your natural lifelong desires, passions, talents and potential. It will contain a harmonious mix of purpose, development, challenge and, through it all, a sense of enjoyment and fulfilment unique to you. The big difference to similar past plans is that you will have come to a satisfying conclusion in your mind on the true nature and role of work – full-time or part-time, paid or unpaid – in your life and whether or not it really constitutes a key part of your continuing search for life satisfaction and contentment. This sort of planning represents a major shift from the traditional "retirement plans" that have tended to be almost totally influenced by financial planning, as distinct from what you are going to do with life after age sixty. The approach being outlined to you here is based on positive thinking, your strengths, talents and untapped potential that enables you to gleefully look forward to the opportunities of the future.

Reflections on the past will of course always retain their place of importance in your life, as they rightly should, the further you go along your life's journey. But such reflections need no longer be seen solely as wistfully reviewing happier times. Reflection also has an important role to play in formulating your desires and decisions on ways in which you want your life to keep on growing.

It isn't just about you of course. Family and all those people you have loved being with outside of your working life assume a new significance. They can still be the strength of your life, people who will always love and respect you. They are likely not only to encourage you to get out there and enjoy life, they may actually be relieved and delighted to see you do so. They want you to live a long, healthy and happy life and be their strength for many more years to come. They certainly don't want you to be bored, listless and frankly a pain in the whatever.

Ok that's enough to get your thinking started and your creative juices flowing. Let's have some fun planning for a life that should essentially be fun, enjoyment and pleasure. Yes including some laughter and frivolity but, more importantly, a life of continuing purpose, value, stimulation, satisfaction, a life that enables you to continue being the person of worth that others have always appreciated about you.

The Worm Has Turned

There are some historical reasons – and also social beliefs – that have greatly influenced the way people today still think about retirement. Historically German Chancellor Otto Bismarck, back in the 1880's, implemented a retirement planning program based on his belief that *"people who are disabled from work by age and invalidity have a well-grounded claim to care from the state"*. Interestingly, Bismarck first proposed the age of seventy years but it soon became settled at sixty-five. The concept of such a pension later spread from there to America and other countries, including Australia.

Laws can of course be changed at the stroke of a pen (or key stroke) – and Australia is looking closely at pushing the pension entitlement age out from 65 to 70. However social presumptions take a lot longer to change in the minds of retirees, of their (adult) children and of the general community, a lot of which is influenced by a largely youth-oriented media.

The changes have not always been so readily adopted into the daily lives of people approaching the traditional age of retirement, especially people providing professional services to the community. Ministers of religion provide a typical example. Ministers have traditionally seen their work not just as a job but as a vocation, their very reason for living. To be told at the age of 65 that you were to be retired, with the perception that you can no longer serve your God and minister to those in need was, to many, too much to bear. Such people often died within months, even weeks, of being retired.

I couldn't of course interview the ones who died early, but I could interview ministers who had survived that transition and were still living happy and productive lives well into their 80's and beyond. The general thrust of their responses was that they had continued on voluntarily doing the parts of their ministry work that they had always loved. One was working with the Alcoholics Anonymous Board, another with indigenous peoples and another was working with helping to resettle refugees who were arriving in Australia. These ministers no longer carried the expectations being placed on them by parishioners, many of whom believed that 'their minister' should be available to them at any time – day or night. Time off for personal enjoyment was not only almost unheard of, ministers themselves often felt a sense of guilt if they took time off to enjoy a personal life interest.

All the ministers that I interviewed had continued working in ministering to people in need. However their new lifestyle was one of freedom to express themselves in their own ways and devote the rest of their lives to causes in which they had always believed and could now undertake in their own way. Ministers are of course only one of so many caring professions and many of you will readily relate to the situations outlined here.

Younger generations have also taken time to adjust to this new way of thinking about what they were calling retirement. If you are now one of the revolutionary baby boomers, you can probably remember when you were embarrassed if your parents wanted to do anything that younger people did – rock and roll dancing, taking up new studies, wearing short dresses or, heaven forbid it, enjoying sex! You expected your parents to "act their age" and grow old gracefully. Senior citizens centres flourished, designed to suit interests more appropriate to older people, with bowls and cards predominating. At home they were expected to be content with gardening, family play and spoiling the grandchildren after picking them up from school.

So retirees themselves tended to believe that the society view was correct, that they *should* grow old gracefully, act their age and generally be seen as quiet, undemonstrative observers of what the younger people were doing.

Suggest that today to anyone over sixty at your peril! The worm has turned. One of the favourite expressions of people who are enjoying their dessert years is to take the assertive approach and seek to grow old *dis*gracefully. We who are enjoying our dessert years now have bucket lists to tick off – anything from travelling the world, or taking a university degree, to skydiving at age 90. We have a spring in our step and a desire to do things that we have for so long seen as outrageous, even mildly naughty! Grey-power movements are gaining strength and demanding to be heard. However I suggest that the jury is still out on the extent to which those demands are being heard, let alone receive social acceptance and become law. The prospects are increasingly getting better as the power-brokers themselves reach their own dessert years.

What is causing this massive and historically relatively sudden shift in the way that the dessert years' people are behaving? Certainly medical advances and the consequent continuation of enjoying a healthy mind, body and spirit are key factors behind our increased life expectancy and our ability to enjoy life for much longer than previous generations. From my perspective as a person who was born just prior to the baby boomer era, the boomer title relates not just to numbers but to a boom in revolutionary social thinking. In their journey through the various phases of life, boomers have left massive changes in their wake, in almost every aspect of social thinking and behaviour. Now they have their sights firmly set on the dessert years as they seek to turn that era on its head, especially with the prospect of it being a much longer and dramatically different era to the retirement years of their parents and grandparents.

Alvin Toffler, in his 1989 book *"The Third Wave"*[2], pointed out that the Agrarian Revolution took 10 000 years, the Industrial Revolution a mere 200 years and the Third Wave was taking a matter of decades. Many would say that since his book we have experienced one, two or even three more revolutionary waves. Somewhere in there, the whole outlook on living all of life to the full – including the dessert years – has become the norm. In much the same way as they say teachers today are training children for jobs that haven't yet been created, so those of us moving into and

---

[2.] Alvin Toffler *"The Third Wave"* Bantam Books, 1989

through our dessert years are recognizing that our remaining years are going to be unlike anything humanity has ever experienced before. With the freedom to live life on one's own terms, it all makes for excitingly new and different times ahead!

Opening The Floodgates Of Your Passions

The true value of leisure lies in the fact that it gives you the opportunity to allow the real you to come to the fore in any way you wish, through experiences you freely choose to create purely for the intrinsic enjoyment and life satisfaction it gives you.

Let me say that again...

The true value of leisure lies in the fact that it gives you the opportunity to allow the real you to come to the fore in any way you wish, through experiences you freely choose to create purely for the intrinsic enjoyment and life satisfaction it gives you.

Leisure has for too long now been treated with disdain – a waste of good productive work time, or something to do when you have got nothing to do. The unrelenting pressures of 21st century living have at last enabled leisure to regain its rightful place in life.

"Free time" is something many of us don't have these days. To define leisure as "free time" is to perpetuate the old perceptions of leisure. A good leisure interest generates energy, no matter how much or how little time the experience takes. Leisure now forms a key part of work life harmony – a concept quite different and much more realistic than the much-vaunted idea of work life balance. Work life balance is about time management in an era where most of us are trying to pack more and more into a finite period of 24 hours, 7 days a week. Work life harmony is about creating a harmonious mix of energy coming in, generated by enjoyable experiences totally unrelated to energy-burning stressful responsibilities, particularly work-related responsibilities. A little renewed energy goes a long way in sustaining the resilience to cope with life. Think then what this powerful redefinition of leisure can mean to sustaining your overall health, wellbeing and life fulfilment throughout your dessert years.

The energy burnt by work and other stress-related responsibilities has to be regularly replaced with new energy. The logical outcome if we don't do so is what has become a major, widespread and insidious problem for businesses worldwide – burnout. In terms of the benefits of leisure on all aspects of your life, including your dessert years, it is important to have some understanding of the nature of burnout and the role of leisure in minimizing the potential for burnout. The symptoms tend to be lethargy, a sense of physical and emotional exhaustion and a loss of interest in work or a sense of lacking accomplishment. Burnout is insidious and, like workaholism, it's only when the damage is already done that the awareness of burnout become apparent. A passionate leisure interest has a powerful, important and naturally effective means of resolving one of business's biggest people issues today – a fact that says much about the potential of leisure in today's society. If the leisure interest you enjoy during your working career is lifelong, your transition from a paid working career to something different could be almost seamless because you have continuing interests that will continue to get you out of bed every day.

Blame it on the Church Fathers

The idea of leisure potentially corrupting the soul goes back to the sixteenth century when religious zealots decreed that work was the only way to salvation and "idle hands were the work of the devil". But it was around the time of the 19th century Industrial Revolution in the United Kingdom that the dichotomy between work and leisure became fully established. The work ethic as it then became known has had a lot to answer for, not because it dignified work but because it demeaned leisure. There are few greater insults than to be called lazy.

Even today the pursuit of leisure continues to get a bad press. It has long found itself hanging around with *slackers and lazybones*, becoming known as something to do when there's nothing to do and generally being regarded as a frivolous waste of productive working time – even a competitor to work. Hard work became the red badge of courage and workaholism a trait of which to be proud. The workplace was – and widely still is – regarded as a place for the tough where the fainthearted might be told *if you can't stand the heat get out of the kitchen*. Depression has for too long been perceived as a sign of weakness to an extent where depressed workers still fear the loss of their job if they say anything about their feelings to anyone in the workplace. Amazingly (well I think it's amazing) even today I still read work-related remarks along the lines of anyone who is looking for work life balance is seen to be 'weak and whining'.

The big change in the image of leisure has come in just the last couple of decades or so. Not because of anything leisure professionals like me have said or done, but because of the massive changes in society, changes that are accelerating exponentially. The stress, pressure, pace, technological advances and other changes that we all experience are having a massive impact on every man woman and child such that we are all looking for coping mechanisms. Much of today's stress comes from changes imposed on us, changes that often we fruitlessly fight against. Anything that would help ease such stress is starting to make the idea of leisure more attractive.

When it comes to retirement planning, the image of leisure has for many people been almost as scary as the image of retirement. The opportunity for leisure has been there all your working life. Whether or not you enjoy leisure interests, you have probably always seen leisure as subservient to work. This implies that having a life of leisure instead of working makes you in some way subservient or less important than those people who are still in the workforce.

The re-energized perceptions of leisure defined here open the floodgates to creatively express any pent-up natural talents and passions, giving you a sense of freedom and self-empowerment that structured work could never provide. And when better can you open those floodgates than when work is no longer the driving force in your life (whether or not you continue working).

I think it's important to spell out in some depth the extent and diversity of benefits one can gain, not simply to get a bit more enjoyment out of life. When I conduct my "Enjoyment Factor" workshops I find that group discussions extend to almost every facet of life – good bad and indifferent, at work, in personal life and in community life, let alone what we do when we are at play. Here are a few features of the leisure experience that I have found particularly important to one's overall life satisfaction.

Nature's stress manager

A really enjoyable leisure experience is in essence nature's stress manager. It transports your mind away from your stresses and pressures for the length of the experience. It's not just that you switch off from your problems but that you positively switch your mind on to an interest so enjoyable that absorbs your mind, body and spirit to the extent that you forget everything else for the time of the experience. Could you possibly even *think* about your problems while you paint a landscape or hit a winning tennis shot past your opponent, or while you are enjoying the glories of a colourful sunset?

The Ripple Effect

Experiences like these give a surge of energy and self-esteem, triggering a refreshed, more positive outlook on whatever you are doing, especially your problems, through the rest of your day and week. The more often you enjoy these *switch off/switch on* experiences, the better are your ongoing feelings about and attitudes towards life, no matter how many problems you are facing.

Skills Development

Any passionate leisure experience is using, developing and building your natural talents and skills. For example if you are an office-bearer in a club you could be developing all or any of organisational skills, project management, delegation, social skills, media skills, team-building. Every skill you develop has value in everything you do at play, at work, at home, or in community life. I am amazed how rarely workplace skills audits ask people to identify talents they use in their leisure interests. Moreover they are talents that they enjoy using and would love any opportunity to use them in their job.

The energy that powers your life

So much focus is placed on physical energy generated by physical activity. That's ok but the physical activity has to contain an essential ingredient – enjoyment. Physical effort that you don't enjoy is probably not going to continue for long (how many fitness machines are re-sold within months of being purchased?) Any leisure experience – physical, mental or spiritual – during which you passionately enjoy creatively using your natural talents and skills (this cuts out passively watching TV or just lying down for a snooze) is energizing. In other words, it generates the emotional and psychological energy to expand and enrich your life, to feel you have grown a little. To me this is one of the key benefits we get from experiencing really enjoyable, creative leisure interests for the sheer intrinsic enjoyment of the experience.

One of my clients put it this way:

"I had been thinking for several years what I can do to bring happiness and had not found something outside of my work and family. I decided to learn the guitar. So my family bought me one for my birthday and now I have finally found something that I not only enjoy (albeit frustrating as well because of course I can't play anything yet) but I have a sense of confidence that this will come with time and practice and I'm thoroughly enjoying the learning experience. "Wow - where did the time go?" happens frequently. I sit down to have a play for a few minutes and before long half an hour or more has passed. It's the first time for a very long time that I now have something to do where I can completely turn off the "work brain" and immerse myself in something completely new and different. And I've given myself permission that I don't have to be brilliant at this as well, just enjoy it". I especially like the sense of self-empowerment triggered by the words "I've given myself permission (to just enjoy myself).

Choices

We learn over the years that life is all about making choices. Where we are and what we do at any stage of life is the result of choices we make. The people we marry, the job we take, where we live and who we spend our time with are all choices. A decision not to choose is itself a choice. Of course circumstances arise that make it difficult for us to choose and indeed much stress comes from feeling we have no choice but to accept decisions made without consulting us. Because I see leisure as a freely-chosen expression of your natural creative skills, our leisure choices are perhaps the last bastion of free choice. No one else can tell you what you should enjoy.

It becomes almost a responsibility to ourselves and our purpose in life to maximize the talents with which we were born, to follow the passions that drive our dreams and to realize the unique potential given to us at birth. Looking at leisure this way, there are a whole host of factors that constitute the sort of leisure pursuits we might 'responsibly' pursue. These include the following:

- Using your unique skills, abilities and talents in ways that totally satisfy your personal unique hunger to grow and blossom into the person you love to be

- Enjoying leisure experiences for the sheer fun you get out of them. No-one else can choose what fun is for you. And it's totally your decision as to whether or not you enjoy an experience that somebody else says they are enjoying.

- The experience is custom-designed by you to suit you. You can multiply any leisure interest by a whole range of factors including the level of excellence you want to achieve, whether to do it competitively or socially, alone or with others and which talents or skills to employ in pursuing the interest. The options become infinite.

- A truly enjoyable leisure experience self-empowers you – you enjoy the feeling of being totally in control and take full responsibility of any outcome from the experience. Often such experiences are the only time you are fully in charge of what you are doing. Even if you enjoy your work you usually have to meet other people's needs and expectations – such as bosses, clients, shareholders, company policies and the marketplace.

- You choose to pursue the interest

    – When you want

    – For as long as you want

    – At the pace you like

    – In the setting of your choice

    – to your chosen level of skill and ability

    – With the people you choose, or alone if you prefer

- An absorbing leisure experience expresses your inner feelings in ways that give you ultimate satisfaction, make you feel good about yourself and about the world around you and enrich your life, your health and your sense of wellbeing

- You become totally absorbed in the experience, lost in a world of your choosing. Such an interest is a positive, healthy form of temporary escape from the problems and pressures of life giving you the renewed energy, enthusiasm and all those other positive goodies you need to make living worthwhile

- It brings out the child in you. Typically, childhood is when we grow fastest, learn more and enjoy living for the moment. When work is no longer governing your life, you can rekindle the best of your child-like (not childish) attitudes towards life, enriched by the experiences of your life to date.

- You allow yourself to be you, not a person you think others might want you to be. So much of your adult life is spent trying to meet the expectations of others. A passionate leisure experience focuses totally on you being able to be the real you. It's a most liberating feeling.

- Your mind, body and spirit are working together. An experience that meets as many of these criteria as possible will give you that magical sense of captivating everything about your mind, your body and your spirit…/soul…call it what you will.

To spark your thinking, here's a few of the enthusiastic responses I have received from clients and subscribers when asked what they do for leisure and – very importantly – how they feel about it and what it does for their lives:

"I enjoy Karate two to three evenings a week I meet friends, exercise and get an adrenalin high sparring with others. Not to mention the confidence I get from knowing I could defend myself against an attacker. Twentysomething? No, sixty plus…"

"Reading, Poetry, playing sport I feel ardently inclined to state that life is amazing when I am enjoying my passions. I feel completely content in the knowing that I am happy".

"I like to lose myself in repairing and making wooden furniture using recycled timbers. I take a long time to complete these projects so they may qualify as antiques. It's my therapy yet at the same time it challenges me with regards to design, measurements, preparing

timber etc. so that it is acceptable enough for my wife to allow into the house. The time in the workshop is "me time" and I appreciate it".

"Cooking. A very relaxing pastime – and I particularly enjoy having dinner parties. I think the buzz of the challenge of ensuring everything is done within the prescribed time is motivating and makes you feel good to have achieved this deadline".

"Riding the Harley (motor bike) is my "me" time. I don't need to explain why I ride a Harley. For those that ride one as well, no explanation is necessary. For those that don't ride one, no explanation is possible!!"

The Power of Passion

My friend Charles Kovess is Australasia's Passion Provocateur. He has been specializing in the field of passion for over 20 years and written two books on the subject as well as many articles. I like his definition of passion: *"a source of unlimited energy from your soul (or 'spirit' or 'heart') that enables you to produce extraordinary results."* There's nothing there about these sorts of interests having to be work-related or age-related. In fact when your passion is no longer harnessed to a job, the sky's the limit.

Think what that offers for ensuring a continuing sense of dignity, respect and life satisfaction throughout the rest of your life and especially when the dessert years unlock your freedom to live life on your own terms.

Let me close this chapter with this remarkable story of faith and courage from a wonderful lady who has long been an online subscriber of mine:

"I love to sing for my soul, paint for my creativity and hike in the woods for my body and spirit. All these activities help me to stay in the moment and practice mindfulness. I have a bipolar disorder. I am normally high functioning and manage to work full time and enjoy a rich family life (which was not always the case in the past). However, I thought for sure with the challenges faced in the past year including a death of a loved one and having to declare personal bankruptcy incurring huge financial loses as well as the loss of our home due to the state of economy would have set off another episode. However, I am staying well, putting one foot in front of the other, taking each day as it comes and managing remarkably well under the stress of it all.

I truly believe that part of the reason I am doing so well is due to pursuit of my interests which I still make time to enjoy outside my work and family life. While involved in the various interests my stress and anxiety diminishes, depression is kept at bay, time flies and I am kept in the zone. It helps to keep me in the moment (when nothing bad is happening) all of which I am so very grateful for. I also joined a Broadway musical choir several years ago. Hubby joined later as well. The choir has grown from 8 to 103 members. The energy amongst the members is so uplifting. It has been a godsend for us both and has really helped us get through this stressful time. We love the music and always feel better after a practice. Plus we have made some wonderful friends from all walks of life. I think my voice has really improved although I am not ready to solo yet. Hubby is a natural and has performed several times as a soloist which I so enjoy".

Where Do You Want To Be?

That is a daunting question. So much life still to come, so much change going on, so much uncertainty in the world. The next section gives you some boundaries within which you can safely think and plan with purpose.

The Real You

The source of your life-hunger (the hunger to continue growing) is found in the real you, the inner self who looks out at the world through your eyes. Who is the real you? While you are in the workforce you'd probably answer by naming the work that you do. It's the sort of answer most people expect to hear. This makes sense because your choice of employment has typically been the major driver behind satisfying your life-hunger. One of the biggest worries you might typically face when considering the prospect of retiring from fulltime employment is not knowing what you are going to say when asked 'what do you do?'. Nobody really likes saying "I'm retired", as though it means you are no longer doing anything worthwhile.

It's likely that your life – especially since the turn of the 21st century – has been one of being constantly under excessive stress, subjected to rapid change, largely unable to control the decisions affecting your work and generally having to conform to what you have seen as other people's expectations of you. All of this happened up to a point where the real you may have had to become something of a stranger to yourself. Not that you have stopped being your real self – the real you has always been the final decider of all your important decisions in life. It's just that you may not have been able to express your true self in so many areas of your daily life, at work and in your personal life. The last thing we do before leaving home for work is to put on a public mask – the bland expression you and everyone else uses while you are out in public. Then there is your business mask, your social mask and all those other masks you have to wear to suit each public situation. When you get home at the end of the day, the first thing you do is take off that public mask and allow the real you to relax in your own way, putting on your own choice of clothes and all of the other things you personally like doing when you are away from the public gaze.

When you look back over the years and compare who you were in your teens and on the brink of entering the workforce to who you are today, these self-perceptions may be very different. The storms of life have battered you incessantly and the real you today is somewhat weather-beaten, but also much stronger and more resilient for the experience. The outer you may look different but the inner you is constant and unchanging. You have worked hard to survive and thrive despite the constant ups and downs to which life and its circumstances have subjected you.

Realizing Your Natural Potential

You would quench or slake your thirst but what do you do with your hunger? It's not a trite question; experts come up with a range of answers including satiate, assuage, quell, satisfy, even quench. I like "satisfying your hunger" because I think in terms of satisfying a hunger pang or discomfort. In this instance I regard discomfort as an uneasy state of mind when you know you have a need to meet but have difficulty finding something that will satisfy that need. It describes the sort of discomfort you may feel if and when your life seems to be stagnating – you feel as if you are stuck in a rut, a feeling that will differ from individual to individual. Only you can decide what will satisfy your particular life-hunger. Only you can weave together the threads to form your own unique way of satisfying the discomfort in your current lifestyle. You are searching for answers that will continue to satisfy your ever-insatiable life-hunger to keep on growing, and blossoming as a unique individual.

The Need for Personal Growth

Your hunger for constant strong personal growth and development is fed by your natural passions, talents and skills. Most of us want to satisfy a lifelong desire to realize our potential. Maslow's Theory on the Hierarchy of Needs[3] gives a good example of the types of hunger that we feel. Maslow describes various stages of hunger - the basic physiological hunger for food, the hunger to be safe and to love, the need to enjoy a sense of belonging and a desire for high self-esteem self-confidence and respect by and for others. All of these needs are vitally important but it's what Maslow sees as the ultimate hunger - self-actualization – that is relevant here.

It's important to recognize just how unique the real you is. You are different to everyone else in your neighbourhood, your city or your country. You are in fact different to everyone else in the world and to anyone who is born before or after you. The obvious differences are of course in the experiences you have had through your life and your unique perception of everything around you. Your individual set of experiences will have a huge impact on your personal perceptions and planning for your dessert years.

Public perceptions of what "retirement" should be do not reflect your idea of how you want to enjoy those dessert years. The main factor about what makes you different is found in your unique mix of talents, passionate interests and the potential these natural assets open up for you. And your assessment of just what those talents, passions and potential may mean to your life, especially for the enjoyment of your dessert years, will be a major factor in the value of this book.

[3.] Abraham Maslow 1908 – 1970 A Hierarchy of Needs theory

Talents

Recognized definitions of the word "talent" emphasize exceptional natural abilities e.g. *"has a rare talent for music; the play has a cast of immense talent"*. While exceptional talents tend to be the ones gaining public attention, I believe we are all built with unique talents. In my case I have found over the years that I have a talent for intent listening to clients and to do so without judgment of what they are saying, a talent for public speaking, a talent for writing, a talent for eye-hand co-ordination shown as developed in various ball sports including golf, field hockey and tennis. In none of those would I be regarded as having exceptional talent that would make me a celebrity – though I am very proud of my achievements in various professional and personal fields where I have applied and developed my talents. To that extent (at least!) you were born with unique talents that have got you to where you are today or are at least the sort of talents that enable you to follow and develop your personal passions in life.

Strengths

Your developed talents become your strengths and your strengths are found in your differences to everyone else and what those differences bring to everything you do and to every situation you face. In this way the concept of talent relates not so much to comparing your talents to those of other people pursuing the same activity as you. Rather it's about the different (unique) ways you in which you use those talents, the benefit of those differences in your own self-growth and in how differently and effectively you contribute your talents to the needs of other people and to society in general. It's by expressing your differences that you can continue to help to make a worthwhile contribution to the world during your dessert years, whether or not you get paid for your efforts.

When it comes to enjoying your dessert years, the most important change here is the release from the strictures and structures of a working career. You will be able to freely enjoy assessing, using and developing that mix of talents that set you apart from everyone else in the world. Even if you decide to keep on working for payment to a large or small extent, you will be focusing your efforts on actualizing those talents and passions that you want to use, develop and enjoy on your own terms, rather than kowtowing to the wishes of other people.

Be the best that you can be.

I see the desire for self-actualization as the ultimate hunger that you want to feed, a hunger that certainly doesn't diminish in your later years. It's a hunger satisfied only by expressing the real you in ways that make you feel that you are being the best person you can be. You will always, consciously and subconsciously, want to express yourself in ways that maximize your desire and potential to grow as a person.

Self-actualization expressed in this way comfortably describes the potential that my concept of leisure aspires to realize, including:

- The realization of your full potential, of your true self, through creativity, independence and spontaneity,

- The process of establishing yourself as a whole person, able to develop your abilities to understand yourself. Who you are is much more than just what you do for a living,

- Your desire to use all your abilities to achieve and be everything that you possibly can,

- Growth towards fulfilment of your highest needs; those that deepen what life means to you,

- And self-actualizers tend to be highly creative.

Certainly it forms a key part of your desire to build an effective transition from a work-limited life to a leisure-unlimited life in which you can continue to enjoy opportunities for your self-actualization.

Your Latent Talent

Surprise yourself

You decide to go along to your son or daughter's sports club annual general meeting to show some moral support. By the end of the meeting you find yourself appointed to a key position in the club's management. You could even be the new President or Secretary. You are stunned and overwhelmed because you have never done anything like that before. By the end of the first year of being in your elected position you had become an experienced event manager, social organizer, delegator, newsletter writer/editor, media liaison officer, meeting manager, or any of a range of other roles expected of a club office-bearer. You did it all so well they have re-elected you the next year, perhaps even elected you to a more senior position! And you love it. This is a classic illustration of the latent potential that is dormant within all of us – the potential we don't know we have until the right set of circumstances arise in which those skills are brought to the fore.

In your life so far you have probably found, developed and enjoyed skills that still give you immense satisfaction, be it through your formal employment, your leisure pursuits, at home, or through your involvement in community affairs. You would also have discovered talents and passions in your youth, probably as a teenager that you decided – or were told – wouldn't earn you money. So you didn't pursue them any further once your time got swallowed up by your working career, general demands of the establishment and support of your family. You were too busy generally trying to meet a wide range of expectations placed on you by others.

Your time to shine

During your dessert years you can re-discover the talents and passions of your youth, aided by the depth of your life's experiences and related skill developments over your adult years. Not that you would necessarily go back to exactly the interests you had all those years ago. If, for instance, you used to play the piano, you might like to use your musical talents in other ways such as learning the guitar, form an old rockers band or join a community choir (or play the piano for a choir). If those interests involved physical activities, there are plenty of people enjoying their dessert years hiking, climbing, running marathons and the like. When undertaking physical activities it is of course always advisable to have the guidance and support of appropriate health professionals, whatever your age may be.

It's all about timing.

You've probably heard the expression, '*when the student is ready, the teacher appears*'. It's one of life's strange quirks that when you are interested in and destined to do something you don't know much about, somebody with relevant expertize unexpectedly happens to come on the scene to guide you through, teach you the ropes (often in equally unexpected ways) and open up a new and often very divergent use of your natural talents, passions and potential. This has probably already happened to you at least once in your life and your dessert years offer a great chance for it to happen again.

When a door closes, a window opens

These types of unexpected opportunities are more likely to arise when you are open to finding something new and fresh in your life. The transition from fulltime employment to a life lived on your terms offers fertile ground for such an enriching experience to occur. When doors close, other doors seem to open – *as long as you are alert and looking for those doors to open*. Some call it fate, others call it the universe, and some say that God arranges it all. Nature abhors a vacuum and that applies equally to any time in your life when you are hungering for something new and different. What will feed your hunger can only be determined by you.

Of course you don't have to simply wait and hope for something to fall in your lap. You can opt to try new and exciting things that you have never done or experienced before. That doesn't mean you have to go to climb Mount Everest to see if you like it. Just take a peep outside your comfort zone and investigate pursuits and experiences that are outside the safe square of your life's experiences and interests to date. The important thing here is to believe in the process.

This could be the greatest opportunity of your life

Leaving the strictures of a structured working lifestyle is giving you what may well be the greatest opportunity of your life to find a new lease on life, a new world, one that will bring a new side of yourself to the fore. It could expose you to experiences you never dreamed of, bring a new sense of absolute enjoyment of life. It could also unlock a potential you never thought was in you but which nature always knew you could achieve.

Lose Yourself To Find Yourself

When you lose yourself in an interest you love, you find yourself. That statement has become the very core of my lifestyle mentoring business. When you become completely absorbed in an interest that you passionately enjoy, you lose all awareness of events around you and even of the passage of time. You allow yourself and your talents to come to the surface and to be expressed in ways totally unique to you. The more passionate, fulfilling and mind-consuming the interest, the more life-enriching it's likely to be.

During these experiences you undergo a transformation. You come alive, allowing the real you to come to the surface. Tensions, stresses and pressures are eased; problems are put to one side for the time being, perhaps re-emerging later as being far less serious than you thought initially. Your talents for creativity and innovation are set free and your mind opened to thinking outside the box.

Finding Yourself

What's going on during the experience? Your imagination is let loose to allow ideas to flow without any sense of judgment on their potential to be realized or not. If these experiences come naturally and often to you in your work as well as in your leisure, you have indeed been living a fortunate life so far. Being able to live the rest of your life away from required work and spend more time living life on your terms allows you to lose yourself in order to find yourself more often. You can throw open the doors to a new life. The world today dearly needs people to pursue their passions, develop their talents and explore the unknown, so don't hold back.

Life on your terms

Only by fully understanding who you are, embracing the talents you possess and knowing what you want to get out of the rest of your life are you truly going to be able to live a satisfying life on your terms. It doesn't mean that you must forget or ignore all that you have previously done with your life. That has been and always will be your life and you should be proud of your achievements to date. It's just that now you have the incredible opportunity to re-discover and appreciate all that is possible for a person of your specific talents, passionate interests and life experiences to achieve without being required to limit your ideas to ways of making money only.

The Power of the Enjoyment Factor

Suppose you are asked to undertake two tasks. The first one you thoroughly enjoy. You find yourself leaping into it with gusto, allowing all of your creativity to flourish, your skills coming to the fore. Your feelings are positive. Your productivity level is high. The second task you intensely dislike. Your enthusiasm level drops, you look for ways out of it, and you give it minimal attention. Your feelings toward this task are negative. Your productivity level is significantly lower.

The difference here is the enjoyment factor. Enjoyment makes you feel good about yourself, impacting positively on your thinking, actions, hopes and expectations. Enjoyable experiences can have a huge impact on your quality of life and lifestyle.

Enjoyment

Enjoyment is a life-expanding experience. Take for example the surprise musical treat the commuter passengers got on their morning train in Perth Australia when a group of young people led a sing-along. Even the most stoical passenger would have felt the presence of the enjoyment factor in this experience. The song ended with rousing cheers and applause from passengers. You can be sure that their sense of life enrichment went well beyond the train trip, lifting their day and those of the people with whom they would have come into contact during that day and beyond. The infection of enjoyment is one of its most powerful characteristics. And music seems to have that innate ability to lift people.

Enjoyment has an active ingredient that adds spice your life. The buzz that you get out of an enjoyable experience lifts your sights and inspires you into some degree of greater action. You could see it as a call-to-arms.

Enjoyment has to be present for the experience to be meaningful and enriching. You can be dragged to water but it's the enjoyment factor that causes you to drink of the experience and to later remember it fondly.

Enjoyment is a creative experience with three phases. Think for example about the last time you went to the cinema:

- o There was the planning and the anticipation – deciding what film to see, booking the seats and traveling with expectation to the cinema.

- o Then there was the actual experience of watching the film – the enjoyment you got out of escaping from the realities of life for a couple of hours.

- o Finally there is the reflection phase – memories that can last a lifetime or at least for a while as you muse on the satisfaction you got not just from watching the film but from all three phases of the experience.

You can apply this "three-phase" thinking to virtually any enjoyable experience. Travel is another great example. Enjoyment is an experience that you create. Fun, laughter and the general feeling of pleasure and contentment are sensations that follow as a result of the enjoyable experience you created.

Enjoyment is the key to realizing your full potential. Joy enables you to blossom into the person you feel you were always capable of becoming.

The Power of Play

We tend to underestimate the power of play. Many of the most powerful features of a passionate leisure experience are typically first learned during yours early years of play – creativity, imagination, challenge, curiosity, lack of fear to give something a go without worrying whether or not it succeeds. Creating elaborate sandcastles at the beach, making up the rules of a game, with frequent changes to cope with unanticipated disagreements and complaints from other children involved in the game. And of course saying "yes I can" to any request to sing, dance, paint, draw, act or any other request to be creative. I am sure you heard the story of the child who said she was drawing a picture of God. When told that no-one knows what God looks like, she replied "they will in a minute!"

What was happening in all of these examples was the play was teaching imagination, creativity, social interaction, rule-making (leading to adult tasks of policy making and even writing constitutions, motor skills, decision-making...the list is endless. In just the five years from birth to starting school a child who enjoys these sorts of experiences is equipped with most of the basic skills of life.

Those first five years are probably the most dramatic years of growth and development. This fact is also perhaps the most powerful reminder that we learn so much more and with greater effect when the teaching process is enjoyable and includes plenty of fun and creativity. This is a valuable lesson for life and especially for your dessert years when you can once again have the freedom to freely express yourself as you did in your childhood. The rich difference in your dessert years is that you have the benefit of your life's experiences on which to creatively express your favourite talents, skills and interests.

I once saw a sign on the fence around an urban school "no unauthorized play permitted". How dare a school – a school! of all places! – should put that sort of a perspective on the sheer unadulterated, joyful and unbridled experience of play, be it by children or by adults. I understand the school's legal concern about insurance risks if a person gets injured, or worse, outside school hours on the premises. But any sign on a school property that inhibits the joy of play surely goes against every principle of the aim to teach children the art of learning.

The message for your dessert years?

So much of who you are today can be traced back to your childhood. Your dessert years allow you to play with learning again. You can again enjoy learning, for the sheer pleasure that learning and its uses brings to you and to positive like-minded other people.

Curiosity Is Creative

Curiosity moves us to investigate, explore, test, challenge.... words that, in turn, inspire us to venture into the unknown. Curiosity opens up that magical world of fantasy, imagination, play, doing what you want for the sheer joy of seeing what happens. For many of us our sense of childlike curiosity was drummed out of us once we reached adulthood and was replaced by the busy economy-driven working realities of adulthood. We found ourselves to be discouraged, pressured to conform to what we saw – or were told - as the expectations of others. One of the great joys of your dessert years is the opportunity to re-kindle that childlike sense of curiosity.

Curiosity did not kill the cat

You can continue pursuing familiar interests and pathways or you can be curious about going down a new path. As suggested in Robert Frost's enticing poem *"The Road Not Taken"*:

"Two roads diverged in a wood, and I...

I took the one less travelled by,

And that one has made all the difference"

Rather than go down paths well-worn by the feet of other people, there is much untapped potential that may be discovered by allowing your curiosity to travel down unusual paths or even create a path to an unknown destination never before discovered. The idea of being a pioneer has always appealed to me. Perhaps there is an unknown path that you might be curious to explore.

One of the joys of eating is to be curious about a food you have never before tasted. When the outcome of such reckless bravery is the discovery of a new taste sensation in your life it can open up an exciting new world of culinary delights. The variety of new food tastes that we all can enjoy today is just one of the wonderful outcomes of having people from other exotic cultures all over the world who have come to our shores to live. Like trying a new food, it's no good just thinking about what it might taste like. You have to try it. Now imagine transferring the curiosity about an untried food taste to being curious about an interest that others have said is great but which you have never tried. Some examples: have you tried genealogy – searching family history information, often going back centuries. learning a musical instrument such as the harmonica. the oboe, clarinet, violin, or trumpet? Perhaps set up an animal sanctuary, go back to university to do a course for fun, give a TED talk, take formal singing lessons, establish a themed photograph display on, say, unusual public signs, build a model railway that you can show to under-privileged children... the possibilities are endless.

Curiosity and reward go hand in hand. The first reward is one of satisfying your curiosity, a warm feeling that you at least gave it a go, irrespective of the outcome. A decision to go further opens up scope for further rewards through greater understanding of a world wider than you have previously experienced, breaking through to a new comfort zone and so on. Whatever the subject of your curiosity and whatever the outcome, you have learned something you didn't know before – in itself a rewarding experience.

All the world's great advances – medical and otherwise – began with a sense of curiosity about the unknown. Try being more curious about everything going on around you. What might you do in the area of say the arts, birdwatching, fund-raising, nature studies, astronomy, working with homeless people or other area of human need? Who knows where it might end?! As you move into your dessert years, be prepared to try new experiences to see if you like them. If you don't there's nothing lost. But if you do... the rest is up to you.

From Acorn To Oak

Imagine that you were born as an acorn. You are growing nicely into a healthy young sapling. Then someone asks you what you want to be when you grow up. You proudly tell them you want to be a strong oak that everyone admires. *"That's nice...but why?? Oaks don't make money. You should become something like an almond tree or a fruit tree or a grape vine"*.

For the young oak sapling it just can't happen. Its natural destiny will always be to become a mighty oak, providing home and shelter for birds and taking its rightful place in sustaining its surrounding ecosystem of its flora and fauna. The ecosystem around that tree depends heavily on the presence and health of that tree. We are all born with a specific purpose but in the case of us humans we are so often diverted from our destined course into trying to become fruit trees instead of the oaks we were meant to be.

When I was nine years old, my friend used to love collecting rocks and putting them in a straight line on a shelf in his cubby house. The display grew over the years and I was always fascinated by his passion for what at the time I saw as silly little rocks. Here was a boy who, while he also had the usual boyhood interests, had a dream very different to most boys at that age.

His dream was to become a geologist. This goal eventually required him to do a science degree which caused him much grief. He failed various subjects along the way but pressed on undaunted, his dream always firmly set in his mind. To this day I can still vividly recall the joy in his life and that of his parents when he finally managed to graduate. That little boy who loved collecting rocks was now a fully-qualified geologist. He went on to spend his working life travelling to some of the most exotic parts of the world – and working in some of the toughest natural environments imaginable. His life is a classic illustration of the acorn to oak analogy. He was born with the natural talents and passion to become a geologist. While he had to face a few storms to fulfil his natural potential, he was always going to get there, do well and be admired as a person who has achieved a great sense of self-worth.

Economic realities

Were it that we could all do that! More than likely you are one of the silent majority who finds that life gets in the way of achieving your natural –born destiny. When you reached adolescence (the sapling stage of life) you were faced with the fact that you had to develop a life based on achieving a lifestyle that centres on paying the bills (plus some left over). Whether or not you could do so and still follow your natural growth pattern depended on the whims of the employment world. Often you had to become a *square-peg-in-a-round-hole* in order to get a job that enabled you to feed, house and educate the family and yourself.

Old oaks

We are in an age where people are using new ideas and innovative thinking to create new industries to serve a rapidly changing society. The time-poor industry is full of older people establishing a new – and often financially-successful life in which they provide services while really enjoying what they do, feel they are helping others and are in charge of their own destiny. Dog-walking, gardening, tidying, repairs and maintenance, managing people's homes, gardens, pets etc. while they are on holidays are just the tip of the iceberg businesses that are the product of self-driven thinking.

This provides amazingly fertile ground in which you can still achieve something of your acorn-oak destiny, one that allows you to re-discover the young sapling in you but in a way that still values and utilizes the best of all you have since learned along the way.

Rooted in nature

We humans are a part of, not above, nature. I believe we should look to nature for guidance in the evolution of our personal lives. I wrote the following a couple of years ago at the request of my good friend Keith Ready who published it as an *InspirEmail* in his online *Gifts of Inspiration program*.[4]

[4.] http://www.agiftofinspiration.com.au/

You are Part of Nature

There I was in the midst of a beautiful park setting... quiet, birds busily making a life for themselves and perhaps for their young, trees rustling gently in the breeze and a sense of peace that only nature can create. Yet the more I listened the more I heard, the more significant became the insignificant and the more I saw what I don't normally see.

In my daily life this is not a world of which I am a regular part. Life for me is the concrete jungle of artificiality, of changing technology, of hurrying people and, to quote the Australian poet Banjo Paterson, 'the ceaseless tramp of feet'.

Yet I was being inexorably drawn into this quiet purposefulness going on around me. Each part of this fascinating flora and fauna jigsaw had a part to play in creating a wonderfully colourful natural ecology, supporting each other and working as one. I was almost forcibly reminded that I am a part of nature, neither a foreigner nor an interloper, that I have a part to play in sustaining, nurturing and harmonizing this symphony of life.

I was surrounded by an aura of family...mother nature calling me home, welcoming me without judgment, putting loving arms around me, offering natural peace of mind, resilience to cope with the winds and storms of life, re-instilling in me a sense of compassion and understanding, even when she knew I have not always been loyal to her.

The peace of nature brought me back to the person I was born to be, endowed with a unique mix of natural talents, passions and potential intended by mother nature, or God or whomever. A journey back in time, unearthing the me I had once loved to be, desires left behind years ago...unfinished, undeveloped and unsatisfied. Tools that had been given me to make my contribution to the natural ecology of human achievement lay in the dust, unused.

Yet the promise that only nature can bestow meant that these tools, these talents, these passions, these desires were not dead, but merely buried, dormant. Like green shoots rising from the ashes of a fire, they needed simply the gentle rains of new human interest and re-kindling of old passions to sprout, grow strong, flourish and blossom.

Take time out to go back to nature, to your roots and your favourite habitats. Revisit, unearth and rekindle your dormant passions and take your natural and rightful place in the ecology of human progress, development and achievement.

The Roles Of work And Leisure

Let's play opposites for a moment. If I said white, you'd say black; if I said outside, you'd say inside; if I said up, you'd say down. If I said work, would you say leisure?

Your leisure interests have probably always played second fiddle to work ...they've been more like the space between the music notes – vitally important to the sense of what makes music wonderful, but not what everybody remembers. Is this unexamined view of leisure going to keep you getting up every morning in place of a working life? Is it going to satisfy your hunger for the dessert stages of your life?

Nature doesn't distinguish between work and leisure

Society created an artificial distinction between work and leisure, particularly in the last couple of hundred years or so when the concept of the work ethic gathered strength. It soon became entrenched as the only way to achieving prosperity, personal dignity and corporate success. It has taken many subsequent generations and the unrelenting stresses of today's society to allow 'leisure' to start recouping something of its historic glory as the way to achieve the wonders and beauty of creative thinking, innovation, invention and the richness of music and the arts.

Nature isn't concerned with whether you develop your natural-born talents through work (serving work-related goals) or leisure (serving personal goals). Nor does nature recognize any change from a life based around work to what we humans decreed as 'retirement'. Nature's intention is simply that, whatever you do, you should keep feeding your hunger to move forward in life.

Leisure also has a role to play in cutting through any division you have felt between the physical and emotional aspects of your life, your health and your sense of wellbeing. Your favourite leisure interests can help you to curtail and overcome many of the emotional ills generated in a stress-ridden life.

A personal example – musical redemption

The best example I can give you is a personal one that took place some years ago during a highly-stressful period in my own life. The stress grew over a period of some six months or so – the combination of a rapidly-failing relationship and workplace issues that resulted in me losing my job. Each on their own was an intolerable situation; their joint impact over a period of months caused my self-confidence and self-esteem to plummet to rock-bottom.

At perhaps my lowest ebb I was invited to join a choir. Much as I loved singing, I had not been involved in a choir for some years and was in no frame of mind to sing for or with anyone. I was wallowing in a good dose of self-pity. The requests persisted and eventually I relented. I hoped it might at least give my mind a break from my problems for a couple of hours. On arriving at my first rehearsal session the choir director said – in front of the whole choir – "Welcome Peter! We are so glad you are here and we look forward to having you involved in the choir". Everyone burst into enthusiastic applause. A small thing perhaps but a very significant one to me – it was something I hadn't experienced for a long time. Over the coming weeks I began to find myself enjoying singing in the choir. Soon the director was telling me that I was doing well and making a strong contribution. "Keep up the good work" was a beautiful thing to hear again.

I found my self-confidence and self-esteem to be steadily growing – and not just while actually singing in the choir. My dark world was brightening and I was starting to look at my problems differently. There was a ripple effect of new confidence flowing through to everything else in my week. When I tell that story in speaking engagements I often say "the guy standing in front of you today owes a great deal to my decision to join that choir – and to the lady who nagged me for a few weeks to join them. Today I belong to two choirs, both of which continue to be a vital and energizing part of my week, contributing significantly to my revitalized ability to continue flourishing, developing and blossoming.

Whatever you passionately enjoy for its own sake has great potential to turn your life around in many ways well beyond simply the pursuit of that interest.

Matured–Aged Workers

From time to time I help a business colleague out who operates a book sales and distribution business. My job is to pack and seal boxes of books, listed on an invoice, and prepare the necessary paperwork for them to be delivered to bookshops or newsagencies around Australia. Simple as it may sound, attention to details is a critical factor, combined with the need to be sure that the job is done right and that it can be done without supervision (there are only a handful of people involved in the business). My friendship with the owner has little to do with why he engages me to do the work. More importantly he values my life-long experience to see a job for more than it immediately appears. that I can make sound judgments as needed, he can rely on me to get the job done on time, that I don't slacken off when he is not around, I take orders easily, I have the nous to respond in a mature way if something out of the ordinary happens, plus many other factors that cause him to know that he has one less thing to worry about in his busy day. In short he greatly values my maturity.

It's a great personal example of a mature-age person successfully – to me and to the owner of the business – performing a job for which I have had no previous experience and which is totally unrelated to my life-long working experience and known talents.

My credentials for this job were essentially those of my mature age and life experience.

This story is taking place in an era of a rapidly-ageing workforce where it is still a major battle to convince employers to employ mature-age workers. Fortunately, my book distribution friend is by no means alone in understanding and increasingly using the experience, reliability, insightfulness and commitment of mature workers. Business is crying out for experience, commitment, stability and enthusiasm in its workforce – characteristics that are well-developed in mature workers like you wanting to continue your life-hunger in your dessert years.

Positive Human Behavour

Obviously you want to enjoy a positive outlook on life. Not just in relation to any given day or experience but also in having a positive belief that your life is overall one of 'the glass being half full' and continuing to fill.

My many years of experience working with people in the development of their favourite – often passionate – leisure activity, recreational or sporting interests has taught me five principles of positive human behaviour. Whenever you are experiencing any one of them, the others almost automatically follow, like a chain reaction.

The sequence is as follows:

- Your mind is processing information at a fast rate, with purpose and enthusiasm to effectively produce a desired outcome

- There is an energy driving the process. This energy is more of an emotional energy than a physical one. The sort of positive energy you have in mind when you hear someone say, "I love his/her energy"

- The experience increases your self-esteem, self-confidence, self-belief and a strong sense of self-worth

- The experience is life-expanding, life-enriching, giving you the sense that you are continuing to grow and develop in so many ways as a person

- The effect is infectious – people in the immediate surroundings feed off your positive energy

When strong mental fitness fails

Any experiences – at work or in personal life – that reflect all of these features provide a wonderful basis for sustaining mental and emotional energy and strong mental fitness.

This message becomes patently obvious when you consider the reverse, where negative human behaviour is happening. A senior business client of mine was feeling the negative effects of the then global financial crisis. He was looking over his shoulder constantly, aware that his very senior job may become so much flotsam and jetsam to be cast overboard by the company to lighten its financial load.

"Peter, I think you are on to something with these features of positive human behaviour", he mused. "In my case, however, I am experiencing them negatively and with a totally reverse series of effects." He went on to explain his workplace situation which was giving him a growing sense of depression. He saw himself experiencing negative human behaviour, characterized as follows:

- His mind was working sluggishly, with unclear purpose and confused outcomes being sought

- His energy levels were way down

- His self-esteem, self-confidence and self-belief were low and falling

- He felt his life was stagnating which in effect meant he was going backwards

- He could sense that his depression was affecting staff confidence and morale, causing their work, in turn, to become sluggish, lose energy and so on. He was caught in a negative spiral which could in itself have a major impact on his ability to retain and work productively at his job.

Cooking up a storm

He remembered that he had always had a great love of cooking for his family, he loved cooking up a storm. He hadn't done so for a while and agreed to try doing so again. It was what I refer to elsewhere as a " switch off and switch on" opportunity - switching off his mind from his negative work-related problems and switching it on to a positive interest, i.e. to enjoyably create great meals for the family he was working so hard to support.

In circumstances like those of my client, it becomes necessary to go outside the stress-generating cycle to find the required unique emotional release. Such experiences are often found in leisure interests totally removed from the working environment. These occasions don't of themselves turn negative thinking around. But you might look at them as the tugboat that gradually turns the Queen Mary of depression around. Over time my client started to see the world differently and more positively (like my story about when I joined the choir). Once the positive momentum started building up, so did his confidence, self-esteem, energy and all the other positive behavioural factors I've listed. He hasn't looked back since and is once again enjoying renewed success in his business career.

The moral of the story

I am telling you this story because it can do much to get you in the right mental frame of mind now, as you consider making the transition from the main course of your working life to the dessert years. You generate the positive energy needed to face the fears you might presently be experiencing about a future for you that is no longer centred on a workplace. Your dessert years will allow you the time to experience that sort of positive behaviour as often as you wish without the ties that work obligations create. Any favourite, freely-chosen, mind-absorbing leisure interest can do it. The emphasis is not on whether the interest is physical or mental but on the degree to which it absorbs your mind and spirit in ways that make you feel good about yourself, about what you are doing and the direction in which you are heading.

Staying Mentally Fit

Your mind governs everything you do. A fit mind is therefore at the core of your total health, wellbeing and your ability to do everything you want to do at work, home and at play. In an era where the mind is under more – and more constant – stress and pressure, people are cracking under the mental strain of it all. But for many people out there the words 'mental illness' or even 'mental health' still have a stigma attached to them. People in general fear a diagnosis of being mentally ill.

Mental fitness, like physical fitness, is a much more palatable term. Both terms represent a state of health to which we aspire, that relate to the desire and ability to cope with everyday life, plus something in reserve to be accessed when under abnormal pressure. While we continue to value and aspire to good physical health in our dessert years, we do tend to become fearful of any decline in our mental fitness and especially the risk of Alzheimer's disease.

There are plenty of well-known ways in which you can stay physically fit and healthy into your later years. But it's not so readily clear what you should do to stay mentally fit and healthy. While physical abilities may diminish as the body ages, sustained strong mental fitness is a constant lifelong need. Leisure, as I have defined it in this book, has an amazingly powerful, enjoyable, positive and influential role in keeping you mentally fit and healthy for life. Staying mentally fit, in turn, has a major role to play in helping you stay physically fit and healthy.

The World Health Organisation defines health and wellbeing as "*the* state in which *the individual* realises his or her own *abilities*, can cope with normal stresses of life, can work productively, and is able to make a contribution to his or her community"

Vic Health – the Health education arm of the Victorian State Government here in Australia puts it this way, "the embodiment of social and *emotional* wellbeing – not merely the absence of mental illness. Mental wellbeing is a *dynamic* state in which people are able to *develop their potential*, work *productively* and *creatively*, build *positive* and respectful relationships with others, and *meaningfully contribute* to the community".

Mental fitness and wellbeing enables you to express your natural-born talents through the creative pursuit of passionate interests, at work and in your personal life, and mixing often with positive, like-minded people and to get everything done in your busy schedule and have mental energy to spare.

Leisure interests as discussed in this book therefore clearly fit well with the various official definitions of mental wellbeing. I tend to emphasise non-competitive interests such as music, the various forms of the arts and crafts, photography, genealogy, or helping others. If your preference is a competitive interest, you need to ensure that fun is a big part of the experience. Going to the gym regularly is good for physical energy but will only sustain your mental energy in the long term if you really enjoy what you do there. In other words, the long-term benefit is in the enjoyment factor. The idea is to generate positive mental energy – to energize you and not to stress you out.

There are many things you can do in your normal daily life to stay mentally fit and healthy throughout your dessert years. Here's a few for you to check off against your current lifestyle. I include some that relate to work (or employment), in case you see yourself continuing to work part-time or full-time during your dessert years:

- Mix with positive, like-minded people with whom you share a non-work creative interest, such as your church community, a sporting club, a choir or other musical group, astronomy club, or volunteers with whom you share serving in a worthy cause

- Have an array of "complementary-opposite" interests, Complementary –opposite interests are those that, by virtue of their very different nature, trigger different emotionally-healthy effects on your mind, body and spirit. Examples include:

    - Indoor interests ...and outdoor interests

    - Using your hands... and using your mind

    - Engaging in some interests by yourself ,,, and some with others – particularly in a group. You will always need a variety of social networks comprising people with whom you feel comfortable and mentally relaxed

- Combine quiet reflective interests and more noisy, robust interests

- Cultivate a harmonious mix of energising interests that offset the energy-draining demands with which you will still need to contend during your dessert years

- Grow a diversity of relationships networks - not just in business. This point is critical to your continuing enjoyment of life if you are no longer involved in a workplace environment

- Take a pride in yourself – including your diet, your appearance and what you say

- Try to continuously improve yourself bit by bit, The Japanese have a word for it – Kaizen, meaning "a change for the better" but with the emphasis on small improvements often and over time.

- Be kind to yourself - you're ok. So often we give ourselves a hard time in our efforts to feel we are adequately meeting what we perceive are others expectations of us. So often those perceptions are in our own head rather than in the minds of other people. Put more simply, we so often wonder what others think of us when in reality we are usually the last thing in their minds.

[5.] Peter Nicholls "*Enjoy Being Proud of Who You Are – 52 Inspirational Life-skills Messages for Teenagers*", Doctorzed Publishing, Adelaide 2012

- Believing you have an abundant life. This relates to much more than mere money. Maintain an attitude of gratitude for all the ongoing blessings in your life - health, family, friendships, passions, talents, interests…the list should be endless.

- Doing things that help other people feel valued. In my previous book for teenagers, "Enjoy Being Proud of Who You Are"[5], one of the more popular messages I wrote was "if you want to feel better, help someone else feel better". I think that says it all.

- Being aware of your senses and what is going on around you. Mindfulness is the current buzzword for this.

- Imagine that you can step outside of yourself and watch yourself in action. Take notice of any circumstances in which you see yourself as particularly stressed or particularly at peace with yourself. Decide that you are going to be aware of such circumstances in future and the effect they have on your mental fitness.

If you are thinking that "staying mentally fit" implies hard work, the following story might help to allay your fears. A client of mine who did my retirement planning session a few years ago and, with his wife, took a 'sea-change' move interstate, summarizes his dessert years lifestyle plans this way:

"In deciding upon retirement, I thought about three things to satisfyingly occupy my time. The first was just doing things for me. The second was to do things for me that involve other people.

The third was to do things for other people. I wanted to keep in mind my overall philosophy in life of doing no harm to myself, nor to others or to the environment.

So I went back to my childhood for points one and two. I came up with intricate developing and colouring mandalas for number one. I enjoyed playing card games in my teens and early twenties and decided to join the local bridge club. I took lessons and I am now becoming quite proficient. I am enjoying the mental challenges, the camaraderie and the busy-ness of game days.

For three, I looked for some volunteering opportunities and was lucky to be approached to join the Board of a local not-for-profit community service specialising in care and support for the disabled. My business skills and life experiences are proving to be a valuable asset for the organisation."

His lifestyle today reflects beautifully the fact that mental fitness is primarily about focusing on the mind and getting enjoyment out of exercising the brain.

The Hunger To Belong

I clearly recall the day about two months after I left the last of the many offices in which I had worked throughout my working life. I was living alone and sitting at the desk of my small home office. In the dead silence I found myself staring at the wall, thinking if I sat there all day long no-one would know or care. There was no boss wanting a report on his desk by four pm or people coming to me wanting me to do things for them. My kids were leading busy lives and expected me to lead my own life, save for weekend visits, birthdays or the occasional meal invitation.

It suddenly hit me that I had to get off my backside and get out into the world because no-one else was going to do it for me. No longer was I identified by the job that I did – and that seemed to be the main reason people ever contacted me. I had this feeling that during all of my working life it was my work that caused people to come to me and, now that I wasn't working, they wouldn't come to me anymore. I had casual friends through my church and a tennis club, but they had always been there in my life more as part of my diversionary interests. Those friendships didn't get me out of bed every day. The only person who could do anything about my situation was me. I needed to get out there and find like-minded people who would stimulate my thinking, my personal growth and my enjoyment of being alive every day. I needed to make some new connections - or else.

People need people

Whether it is a hunger to belong to a community, a family, the workforce, or a social group, the common factor is a need to socialise with other people. Not just any people, but like-minded people. People who think like you do, share your interests, have a similar education background to you, or perhaps just follow the same sporting team. You want to be with people with whom you can comfortably converse and relate at your level.

When you are no longer in a structured working environment, your ability to satisfy your life-hunger very much relates to the extent to which you can find and share experiences with like-minded others. It is very difficult to meaningfully grow on your own. I am always reminded of this fact in the course of running my one-person business. I feel the need to share business thoughts with like-minded other people before putting new ideas into practice. For some six or seven years now I have been part of a small group of sole entrepreneurs. We meet monthly in each other's homes. Each of us brings to the meeting a project on which we are working. We have very different areas of work but we all value the need to avoid one-dimensional thinking in our respective businesses. It's an incredibly valuable mutual resource for each of us, not just in pure business terms but also in the emotional sense. We share a common desire to grow and to help each other grow. We want not only to develop our businesses, but also to progress our respective personal desires for a fulfilling and meaningful life.

You of course may not want to run a business or even be employed. What you will want and need is to be with other people who motivate your thinking, your interests, your desire to grow as a person, your desire to contribute to society, the desire to be part of growing some interest or project that is bigger than you.

My Story

To help you script-write the story of your life ahead, I thought you might glean something from some of my own story, events that played a major role in my own transition from the main course to the dessert years of my life.

It's important to understand that this story doesn't start only from the day I consciously started planning for my dessert years. In my case it goes back as far as my teenage years. Events happened then that I only now realize shaped my thinking when deciding what sort of dessert life I wanted to lead. This brought home to me the fact that everything I had done over my whole life would impact on my thinking and my continuing hunger to do something of significance with the rest of my life.

When I was fourteen I took up the sport of field hockey and found myself writing the team's weekly match report for the club newsletter. I loved it. At fifteen I became an assistant to the Club Secretary and over the years I rose to various voluntary state and national sports administration roles. By the age of twenty-four I was writing editorials for a church newsletter, succinctly expressing my views on major public issues of the day. I was building a talent for writing that to this day continues to be my main passion. Writing has, to me, become a wonderful tool that I continue to hone in my desire to help as many people as possible around the world.

Seventeen years after I entered the workforce, my world changed in a day.

My curiosity had been aroused by a statement by the then Prime Minister of Australia that leisure may well become the social issue of the 1980's. More than two years later I attended a government seminar in Canberra (where I was living at the time) on *Leisure*. I was totally captivated by the proceedings and soaked up every bit of information I could glean from the day. It led to me undertaking the newly-established Recreation Planning Graduate Diploma at the Canberra University. My passion for this field of study was such that I passed everything with distinction. My desire to learn more about the nature and role of leisure in society and how it affects people has since remained, undiminished.

I found the leisure, recreation and sporting profession to be a profession of passion. As in all true professions, people working in the industry were seeing their work not just as a job but as a vocation, a way of life. Doors began opening for me in very diverse ways enabling me to achieve positions of major responsibility including a term as National President of the (then) Royal Australian Institute of Parks and Recreation, the leading Australian professional association of people working in parks and recreation management and development.

This leads me to another important point for you to note in planning for your dessert years. I did not consciously select options that would ensure I lead a satisfying dessert life. As was the case throughout my working years, most of my dessert years' activities have been the outcome of an external prompt, some going back many years ago. Each time an opportunity was presented to me – often not clearly at first. I had to make a decision whether or not to take up the option. My regular weekly golf game now was not my idea but through the invitation of a friend. At the time the idea did not fit into my arrangements yet it happened and is now one of the joys of my week. Two years ago I was approached to be the Club's President which I accepted and continue to hold at the time of writing. Nor did I have any aspirations to join one of the premier choirs of Adelaide, the Adelaide Harmony Choir until the Choir Director approached me saying the choir was short of tenors. That was four years ago and we are shortly to visit Japan to sing at the invitation of a local Japanese organisation.

Any time you sense an opportunity being presented to you, you should be happy to investigate it fully. But don't just wait for the opportunity to come to you. Get out there now with an open mind for new pursuits that suit your natural talents, passions and interests. Actively seek ideas and interests that might bring you the satisfaction of your life-hunger, irrespective of how much longer you plan to stay in the workforce. If you leave it until you are about to stop working, you may well find yourself very hungry and very unsatisfied.

Your dessert years start as soon as you begin to adjust your thinking from doing what you have to do (supported by what you love to do) to doing what you love to do (supported by what you have to do). Most people start this process from around the age of fifty. That is the time when you start developing the sort of activities that you can continue to enjoy for life, irrespective of any work-related plans.

The Legacy Of Work

The Main Course

So that you can get the maximum benefit from this book, it is important that I dwell for a moment on my approach to the use of the word "work". In daily life terms we have come to know work as *paid employment* or the *sale of our services in return for money*. I don't contest the validity of those definitions in any way. I just want to add a different perspective to the nature and role of work in your life.

I see the traditional concept of work as meeting other people's expectations of you, however you are able to do so and always with a monetary exchange involved in the process. In terms of the dessert years in your life journey, the emphasis changes from one based around meeting the expectations of others to one of choosing to live life on your terms. Work in your dessert years becomes something based around your own choices of how you want to achieve self-actualization. If your motive is primarily financial, it is a matter of paid employment and all that the traditional work ethic involves. And by all means that is a choice you can make if that is your preferred way of enjoying your dessert years. I make no judgment about that option.

Or you can choose to see work as something you do for reasons that are not *primarily* financial but more for the purposes of choosing the freedom to do things on your own terms to achieve your own desires for self-actualization. In my case I chose (now in my 70's) to run my lifestyle mentoring business under the banner of "Australia's People Gardener – *growing better people*". I do so for my own reasons, to live life on my terms, to follow my passions and to cultivate my never-ending hunger to grow as a person. I appreciate payment to me when it comes along but money does not drive my business. I am driven by my desire to give to people who are in emotional need the benefit of the abilities, experience, knowledge and wisdom I have accumulated over my life. That includes the members of my family.

Whether or not you continue undertaking paid work during your dessert years, you can learn a lot about yourself and what drives your life by asking the question "*why do you work?*" Your first answer will probably be along the lines of "to earn money to pay the bills and buy the things I like and need in my life". "And...?" I ask, "Well, I want to be able to pay for my retirement". "And...?" "It gives me the answer I need when somebody asks me what I do for a living". "And...?" By which time you will be starting to feel a little frustrated with my questioning. Well, it is obvious that the money tends to overshadow the lifetime benefits of work to your mental and physical wellbeing – I refer to the emotional and psychological benefits you get from being in the workforce. How your job affects your feelings will reveal a great deal about you, your interests and what drives your life-hunger.

In my workshops, my clients have come up with many interesting reasons why they work once we had broken through the barrier of saying that it's all about the money and the financial benefits to your life. Here are some of them - enough to trigger your thinking and to help you to come up with your own list of benefits to be derived from working other than for the monetary rewards only.

- A sense of belonging to a community of like-minded business people, either in your own workplace, your industry or your clientele. I think that this forms part of almost all of the other factors that I will raise here. They indicate a variety of ways in which we enjoy a sense of belonging – to a job, to the community, to your family and to a productive society in which you feel you are playing a role. It's virtually impossible for you to gain value out of doing things solely on your own. As a sole entrepreneur myself, trust me on this one.

- Acknowledgement by others of your abilities to undertake specific types of work in ways that advance your job and also advance the goals of your employer

- Being part of something bigger than yourself. It's great to feel you are part of a business venture in which you feel acknowledged as an having an important role to play in the business

- Challenges that keep your mind active, alert, enquiring, creative, or innovative and which give you that sense that your life is moving forward

- Commitment to a purpose. A willingness to give your time, talents and energy to a cause you value. I see boredom as largely feeling you are not committed to anything important.

- Autonomy. Having or have been given the authority or flexibility to make your own assessment s or decisions. The devolution of responsibilities and authority to make decisions is becoming more and more essential to the long-term success of a business

- Dignity is a major factor in relation to work satisfaction. The most effective way of explaining the sense of dignity in relation to work is to point to the loss of dignity often felt by a person who has become unemployed and still wanting to regain paid employment.

- Doing something that matters. The feeling that you are undertaking tasks that have value and importance – to yourself and in turn to your employer or clientele

- Giving back to the community. This is a value that has become increasingly significant to me over recent years. I feel valued when I have the opportunity to pass on my knowledge, my insight and indeed my wisdom to younger generations. Some recent research found that, in businesses like McDonalds who greatly value daily customer service, the presence of at least one person over sixty years adds significantly to the quality of such service.

- Having a sense of being in control. There is much of our lives over which we have little or no control – at work and in personal life. However a growing feature of the modern business world is increasing specialization, leading to great devolution of responsibility and authority throughout the organisation. This factor opens up increasing opportunities for professional workers and others to enhance and develop their natural talents and skill on the job and so develop a greater sense of engagement and commitment to corporate goals.

- Impact on others. The organisation and structure of businesses today enables – indeed requires - staff to have a positive and beneficial impact on customers, clients and the marketplace generally.

- Learning and professional development. Work always entails learning in any of a myriad of ways to meet the needs of your job and those of your employer. The hunger to learn never leaves you, just its focus as and when you vary the purpose – paid or unpaid – of your learning,

maintaining connection/interaction with like-minded other people. Whether or not you enjoy the company of your workplace colleagues, you generally enjoy the fact that you all aim to achieve mutual business goals. You enjoy the discussions, agreements, disagreements that are of a professional nature, the mutual determination to achieve common tasks and sharing in the successes (even the failures) of your mutual efforts. Again, you never lose your hunger for sharing interests, challenges and aims as part of a group of like-minded people

- Making a contribution to others. Some of the best feelings any of us can enjoy is the satisfaction of knowing that part of what it means to do well in your work is to know that you have made a contribution to other people, organisations or communities. It's a feeling you want to continue enjoying in whatever you do, paid or unpaid.

- Opportunity to be creative. Few of us enjoy work that requires us to work by rote – having to constantly repeat the same actions with little or no chance to be creative in your way of doing the job well. You were born with a fertile mind, natural talents and passionate interests that you naturally want to make use of in ways that contribute to others and achieve all of the other points listed here about emotional reasons for the work you are employed to do. This is another way where your dessert years can open up the opportunity to live life on your terms and create situations in which you can learn, develop and creatively enjoy your natural talents.

- Professional and social friendships. The work you do has a huge influence on the professional and social networks to which you belong. Those networks generally extend beyond your workplace into professional associations, unions or other networks designed to support development of your workplace responsibilities, interests and goals. Professional seminars, conferences and other off-site work-related gatherings offer great professional and personal stimulation and motivation. This has always been a huge buzz in my own life and I continue to have – even initiate – networks relevant to progressing my lifestyle mentoring passions. This includes enjoying a sort of "emeritus professor" role in the work of what was my professional association during my 'main course' career employment years.

- Valuing your personal abilities and skills. Hopefully you have a job where your talents are appreciated and valued. Certainly all the surveys of what employees want, being valued for one's abilities is as high if not higher than the desire to be adequately paid. Living life on your terms will give you every opportunity to devote your energies to interests in which you know your talents are valued.

- Performance feedback. While formal performance feedback can often be a controversial aspect of paid employment, you will always be alert to any informal performance feedback you gain. I remember whenever a report of mine was approved by the organisation's governing board, my manager would always send me a personal note "well done, keep up the good work". Nearly 20 years later I haven't forgotten! By following your passions in your dessert years, you are likely to increase your chances of getting good performance feedback from those who you help or who share your interest. I love reading the many glowing comments I still get from blog posts I regularly send to my subscribers.

This might be the first time you have closely considered the emotional /psychological reasons why you work. Unless of course you have been faced with the prospect of not working, e.g. if you have at some time lost a job, had a job-threatening injury, or experienced a major life-changing tragedy.

The listed factors drive your whole life-hunger. They will become especially important when you have to decide what you want to do that will keep you getting out of bed each day during the dessert years of your life.

So get pen and paper and set aside some quiet time. Even better, get your spouse or another person who knows you well to work through the exercise with you because they might understand your reasons for working better than you do.

The value of brainstorming

It's important not to depend on just the first rush of answers that come to you in undertaking this process. Like any true brainstorming process, the real benefits of the process come by not stopping when you feel your thoughts are starting to run dry. Push past your first wave of enthusiasm until you get your second wind of ideas and watch the really good deeper thoughts start to come to the surface.

Let's say for example that you included the first eight in your own list:

- A sense of belonging
- Acknowledgement by others of your abilities
- Being part of something bigger than yourself
- Challenges
- Commitment to a purpose
- Autonomy

- Dignity

- Doing something that matters

You will then need to find and pursue freely-chosen interests – paid or unpaid – that give you as many as possible of those emotional benefits in your list. Not only will they be valuable in helping you work out what sort of things you might want to do. They will also help you understand what sort of people you want to mix with to share your interests, friendships you want to encourage, perhaps even where you (and your loved ones) want to live. The benefits you list will help you determine so much more about your own desired identity and what sort of environment you want to create around you that is wider than – or replacing – your present working environment.

Rotary or any other similar community service organisations is a good example of an interest that calls for all or most of the factors I selected - a sense of belonging, acknowledgement of your abilities, being part of something bigger than you, challenges, commitment to a purpose, autonomy, dignity and doing something that matters. Equally it could be something like managing a junior sports club, or taking a role in church management activities. A previous dentist of mine, when he could no longer practice for health reasons, volunteered to spend a month at a time in an overseas tsunami-ravaged country helping to identify people who died, using a dental examination process. Some might suggest he was making an even more important use of his professional talents than he was during his paid employment years.

Having the total freedom to do anything you like is a rather daunting challenge. Your list gives you some guidelines – boundaries if you will - within which you can assess and decide what might realistically express your true self and can meaningfully unlock, develop and maximize your emotional reasons for living. If options don't immediately come to mind, repeat the process whenever and as often as you wish. Not coming up with clear answers straight away doesn't mean the process doesn't work. You are at the height of what is a complex life, a life in which the real you has necessarily been suppressed. Re-discovering the real you, tested and experienced by life's ups and downs is a fascinating exercise in which perseverance may well unearth some amazing facts about who you are and what life on your terms could be like.

I cannot stress enough how important this exercise is if you really want to understand what makes you tick as a unique individual. On my website at www.australiaspeoplegardener.com.au your will find an A-Z list of interests that may help you find new ways of creatively expressing your talents. It is a far more important list than simply some fun things to do, though whatever you eventually choose should indeed be fun. The real value only becomes apparent to you after you have thought through all of the contents of this book, and done the exercise on the emotional reasons you work.

Business wants these benefits now

Today's excellent business leader is adopting some important workforce management practices that can be interpreted as offering a legacy for planning your dessert years. These business leaders are recognizing that to keep the best staff they need to offer more than just the money. The modern workplace vocabulary increasingly includes motivational expressions such as engagement (a feeling that the employee is an acknowledged part of the organisation's drive and development), encouraging autonomous thinking, independence and real initiative. Such managers want staff to feel that they have some control and authority over making their own judgements on their work and that of the wider corporate direction. Such organisations are now often referred to as an "employer of choice" because they operate a workplace culture that appreciates and maximizes the personal potential of their employees.

What does this mean for the dessert years of your life?

The traits that these managers are encouraging for corporate benefit are all traits that drive you as an individual to develop your personal talents and abilities, be it at work or in your personal life. The dessert years become your opportunity to not just do what your boss wants to encourage, but for the interests that *you* want to learn more about and develop for your own professional and personal growth and development. In your dessert years you can decide how important financial reward is to the process but in the end it is about satisfying your own life-hunger. How much time and effort you want to spend on projects that nurture this desire, how much you want to devote to family, to travel, to friends and networks are all decisions entirely up to you to make.

A sense of insightfulness

On top of all this you have yet another even more important legacy from your working years - your well-developed sense of *insightfulness*. It's more than just professional development, knowledge, skills and experience. It's that sixth sense that comes only from years of 'doing what you do well' (to quote an old hit song). It's an asset you have that few people in the younger generations can match!

Personal Relationships

Unless you live life as a hermit, you will have a desire to belong, be it to a partner, your family, friends, a broader community, a business network, or all of these. Such connections are vitally important when enjoying life's main course. They become even more important when it comes to enjoying your dessert years.

I am no marriage counsellor but when the time comes for a couple to make the transition from life's main course to the dessert years, there are some major factors you need to take into account. These factors can be broadly covered under two headings, but they often overlap:

- The physical arrangements of what you each want to do and where you want to live

- The emotional factors arising from the transition.

You will each be writing your respective life stories but you will no doubt want the two stories to interweave in order to create an enjoyable life together. Issues can arise on, say, where you might want to live. It's popular to want a total change to a new living environment, sometimes even a *sea-change* or *tree-change* (move to the country). These are wonderful ideas and perfectly appropriate if you want to start a life very different to the one you have been leading during your working lives. So long as it is something both parties want to do. Different thinking needs to be worked through carefully to avoid the risk of a split where one moves and the other doesn't.

Nor is it simply a physical move. It's a move away from all with which you are both familiar, to a perhaps totally unfamiliar location. If it's a matter of moving closer to your children, are they comfortable with you coming closer to them? They may like their separateness from you and perhaps they are losing the benefits of your present home as a cost-free holiday home. Moving to live near them may also unintentionally inhibit their rightful choice to take up an attractive position for either of them to move elsewhere. Would you still enjoy your changed location if the children moved away? Would you try to discourage them from moving away? These are just some of the things you need to think about regarding where you want to live in your dessert years.

The retired husband syndrome

Until recent times it was common for the husband to go to work and then be faced with the major change of going from fulltime work to no work at all. His wife traditionally stayed home and raised the family. The idea of retirement was foreign to her thinking. The only change she would experience was suddenly having dear hubby around all the time – no longer leaving home after breakfast and returning only in time for dinner. One day he is sticking to this routine and the next day he isn't. It can be quite a shock for both parties. It has often led to what has been called

"The Retired Husband Syndrome" in which the wife, who was hitherto relatively relaxed, now has to put up with the constant and (to her) invasive presence of a husband who feels lost and aimless.

This often created either or both of two major problems:

- The "me too" situation…"where are you going today dear? Can I come too?" This can be as seemingly mundane as the husband wanting to accompany the wife shopping, perhaps for the first time since they were married. Potentially even worse is if he wants to take over doing the shopping! And events like her regular social gathering with her friends, is not only her separate social life, it is part of her personal space – something to be preserved in even the closest relationships

- The way things are done at home. "Why do you do it that way dear? I know a better way".

These sorts of changes in the relationship can at best cause tension, no matter how long and well-established the relationship has been. If this situation goes unchecked it can lead to ongoing stress, separation and even divorce. The time-honoured marriage principle to keep talking through issues of mutual concern applies even more in the dessert years. You want both to enjoy them as the sweet years and not turn them into the sour years.

Of course, today the situation is changing rapidly with both husband and wife often being in the workforce. I am increasingly finding there are more women than men in my retirement planning workshops. It raises some interesting questions that may require the passage of more time before we can come up with some definitive answers. For example, while it may be nice if the two partners decided to make the decision together when and if they would cease fulltime work, it is likely that they will make separate decisions according to their individual situation. Say one is earning significant money and the other not, or one loves their work intensely while the other cannot wait to leave. In this latter situation it could be decided that the significant breadwinner might continue working while the other decides to leave or reduce their work commitments.

Either way, both partners are going to look at all of the issues in this book from a similar perspective – the working person who has decisions to make. So I would suggest that much of the criteria I have given elsewhere in this book still applies. For example, irrespective of when or if one leaves paid employment or not, the principles of shared time and interests and separate time and interests continue to apply.

Whatever your particular marital situation, I have found it important in the dessert years to maintain the sort of personal space principles you and your spouse have enjoyed during your working life. By all means enjoy sharing common interests. Equally essential however is the need for each partner to have time to enjoy their own personal space – times in which they can do their own thing and mix with their own chosen networks of friends and acquaintances.

LAT couples

In most western societies today, around a quarter of the population live alone. This has given rise to the phenomenon known as "LAT Couples" – couples living apart together. Many of the people involved in these relationships are in the second half of their lives and are either divorced or their previous life partner has died. But the pull for companionship is still strong and new partnerships are often formed. Both parties have their own homes which neither wants to forsake. Both parties are comfortable with where they are, the décor and ambience of their home and respect the right of the other partner to feel the same about their home. They enjoy spending time at each other's home, knowing they are able to return to their own home whenever they choose – or whenever the other one decides it's time for them to go home!

Three types of relationships dominate the dessert years

Dependent relationships where couples work best if they are together a great deal of the time.

Independent relationships, where the couples operate best by spending much of their time operating independently in their own space.

And inter-dependent relationships in which there is a harmonious mix of having shared space as well as personal space. This is generally accepted to be the most enduring continuing relationship but whichever arrangement has been comfortable for the both of you in your working lives is probably going to suit both of you best in your dessert years.

And if you are single?

The person living without a partner of course has total control over his or her decisions about every aspect of what constitutes the sweet life for him or her after they have finished their main course in life. While loneliness can bring its problems, the organised and aware single person has the right and freedom to plan life just the way they want it. If it's possible for them to live close to a caring person of significance in their life, so much the better. The issue of developing a variety of social and or business networks is even more important for this group of people, not having the companionship and connection of a partner.

Avenues For Satisfying Your Life-Hunger

There are far more avenues for satisfying your life-hunger over the years to come than could be listed here. Here are some options to help your thinking.

Work

You have an almost unlimited range of options to choose from if you want to continue making paid work a part of your life. For example:

- If you work for somebody else
  - You can opt to keep on working fulltime for as long as both you and your employer continue to see appropriate value in your work
  - Or you might negotiate lesser hours or reduced duties, doing what you are best at doing, perhaps mentoring younger employees

- You no longer have a fulltime job but want to keep using your work skills
  - You might be able to negotiate extending your existing employment but for less hours or in a more specific role

where you and your employer agree that your continuing skills, experience and insights would be mutually beneficial,

- o Or set yourself up as a consultant/mentor/adviser/coach to any business or person who wishes to engage your services. This is not always as easy as it sounds and your success will depend greatly on the degree of passion and sheer perseverance you have for work and the demand in the marketplace for your type of services
- o Or create the job/business of your dreams, one that follows your passions and maximizes your developed talents and maximizes the experience, insight and wisdom you have accumulated over the years. Importantly you must decide the extent to which money is important. Your passion may excite you but the prospect of getting other people to part with their money for the use of your services is extremely difficult to achieve, especially in the short term. Most small businesses fail within a short time for many reasons, not the least being an insufficient sense of passion to persevere when times get tough. If money isn't an important part of the project then go ahead and enjoy giving back to the community what you have learned and doing so in ways that help solve other peoples' problems.

to pass on your knowledge, experience and insights to the younger generation by offering training, mentoring or coaching – e.g. by classes, lectures, seminars or public talks.

- If your working life has consisted of owning and running your own business, you are still in charge of your own working destiny subject to the vagaries of the business world, your personal health and your general capacity and passion to keep working in your dessert years. Just don't forget to maintain interests outside of your working life, care of family, etc.

Leisure

I've already said it all about productive leisure interests being a means to self-actualization in your dessert years. I can only re-emphasize your need to use this book as an ongoing reference source. Keep an open mind to the fact that you have a great deal of latent potential just waiting to be tapped. I believe that's the best way to maximize the limitless nature of your potential.

Of course there are plenty of baby boomers who will always see leisure as doing not much at all – at least not doing much that rivals the value of work. Living life on your terms gives you the freedom to decide whether leisure means a continuing search for self-actualisation or simply doing what you love for no particular reason except for the simple fact that *it makes you feel good about yourself.*

Home Life

Home is where the heart is and that is where you should be best able to allow the real you to surface, relax and grow. How you do that is entirely up to you and I urge you to honour that right, no matter what anyone says. What goes on in your home is private and personal and a time you should treasure.

Community Life

Community means any group of people, location, club or other common linkages that appeal to you. It's whatever constitutes your personal choice of positive and like-minded people. But also it can be a community quite different to those you normally like to be in. A community you want to help in some way, one that could be as close as the people in your neighbourhood or in a third world country on the other side of the world. There are so many people, volunteer projects and community needs out there, all desperately in need of a wide diversity of skills, talents and enthusiasm. Fields such as welfare services, Lifeline call centres, sporting and recreational organisations, fund-raising causes, assisting refugees to re-settle in your community, home maintenance services and library volunteers. There are also organisations that point volunteers in directions relative to their skills, talents and interests. Investigate the internet for guidance.

Teenagers and school children are always prime candidates for soaking up the knowledge and wisdom of older people. This is an area of increasing interest and concern as society battles with the social problems emanating from the pressures of dysfunctional families, parents both working, single parents and the scourge of drug-taking and binge drinking by far too many young people. The wisdom of the elders is a golden asset that just requires the initiative of people to bring the young and the old together in any way possible. If this appeals to you, don't wait to be asked, perhaps even start something that enables new ways of intergenerational connection to be established and developed. It's a potential source of huge satisfaction to all concerned.

Learning

If you are looking to continue working fulltime consider doing some new professional development training or courses of your own choosing. If not, curiosity can still be a great prompt to increase your learning, either in fields with which you are already familiar, or to research topics about which you are curious but of which you presently know little or nothing. Tell others about your findings. Knowledge is only knowledge when others are told about it. Seek out people who would benefit from your knowledge and who are interested.

In another sense we are always learning something new, irrespective of whether or not we are seeking to expand our knowledge and understanding of the world. Any day in which you learned nothing new is a sad day. Many of us see the dessert years as a great opportunity to launch into formal studies, even a University course, or at least a University subject of interest.

You are most certainly never too old to learn. Learning, in all its forms, is very much a core part of your self-actualization process.

Life Experiences

By now you will have experienced much of life in so many of its forms and places. It's doubtful if you will ever reach a stage where you feel that you don't need any more expansion of your life experiences. The desire to keep on growing naturally produces an expansion of your lifetime experiences.

Nor is it always a lineal expansion of your life, through traveling or meeting new people, or experiencing different cultures. There are many emotions – testing, challenging, awe-inspiring, gut-wrenching experiences. Some will be enjoyable, some not so enjoyable, but all of them will expand your life experience to the full. You only get one shot at life, so make the most of it

The Beginning

The book ends here but your new life is now about to begin. A life of potential, opportunity and challenge. A life of looking forward with vision, having the freedom to be the person you want to be and to live life on your terms. The dessert years are a time when you and your loved one can:

- Plan to do all the things your working life restricted you from doing to the extent you have always wanted.

- Become a kid again by seeing the world through child-like eyes, this time with the hindsight of many years of experiences, learning and insight

- Unlimit the limitations you may have felt about your lot in life. Remember the old saying, if you do what you've always done, you will only get what you've always got. If you have always lived a certain lifestyle with little change, now is the time to peek outside your comfort zone and taste some new delights

- Relish the fact that when talents and passions were handed out, nature never saw a distinction between work and leisure interests through which to explore and use those talents. You are no longer bound by the expectations of bosses or clients.

It's your life to live on your terms for your enjoyment. You can creatively express your talents in your own way for your own reasons

- Review your personal list of emotional reasons why you work and use them to help you find new interests, friends and causes. Through these you can explore and develop those reasons without the limitation of having to find the money to pay for mortgages, education and all those other economic reasons that drove you to gainful employment in the first place.

Your life is like a never-ending story, especially if, like me, you feel the urge to leave a legacy of your creative skills, talents and passions to help guide future generations.

Finally, create the dessert life that you want, one that gives you lots of rich, sweet tastes to savour and keeps your life-hunger satisfied. In the final analysis you want to be able to leave the table of your life feeling totally fulfilled and satisfied, content with the knowledge that you prepared and served in your own way a culinary delight containing your particular life ingredients, talents and passions – a masterpiece that that no other person in human history can create or repeat. Ultimately it's all about the joy of never quite satisfying your hunger to live your unique life to the full, doing your thing in your way and on your terms. It's what life was always meant to be about.

About The Author

Peter Nicholls is a Lifestyle Mentor operating as Australia's People Gardener with an aim of *Growing Better People*. His work is based on more than forty years of professional experience working with people of all ages in the planning and development of their favourite leisure and recreational interests, interests that they pursue when they are not at work. His focus brings a unique and positive perspective on life.

Now in his seventies, Peter has all the professional and practical personal experience needed to help people from all walks of life to successfully negotiate one of life's most feared transitions – from work to what we used to call retirement.

Peter focuses on people as part of nature, with natural-born talents, passions and potential. Because nature sees no distinction between work and leisure, Peter looks at life as a birth-to-death continuum of developing one's natural abilities equally at work, home and play. It's an important factor in considering the transition from a life based around work to one based around a life-hunger that knows no boundaries.

Peter established his own lifestyle business at the ripe young age of sixty-three years. He continues to live life on his own terms. This is exemplified in his first book "Enjoy Being You" which he published in 2001. Apart from his passion for writing and helping people to enjoy their lives, Peter is also a keen tenor in two choirs and enjoys his weekly game of golf. Peter has two children, six grandchildren and lives in Adelaide Australia.

www.ingramcontent.com/pod-product-compliance
Lightning Source LLC
LaVergne TN
LVHW051500070426
835507LV00022B/2852